Coffee House Press Selected Works Series :: Two

THIRSTING

EDWARD   SANDERS

FOR PEACE

SELECTED   POEMS

IN A RAGING

1961 – 1985

CENTURY

COFFEE   HOUSE   PRESS   ::   MINNEAPOLIS   ::   1987

Some of the poems in this book were published in the following magazines: *Fuck You / A Magazine of the Arts, The World, Sulfur, City Lights Review, Crawdaddy, The Folklore Center Boat, Earth's Daughters, Pearl, Light Work, Fathar, Yanagi, The Portable Lower East Side* and *Woodstock Times*. Some of these poems appeared in the following anthologies: ALL STARS (Viking Grossman), THE POST MODERNS: NEW AMERICAN POETRY REVISITED (Grove), ANTHOLOGY OF NEW YORK POETS (Random House), and NEW WRITING IN THE U.S.A. (Penguin). Some of these poems appeared in the following books: PEACE EYE (Frontier Press), EGYPTIAN HEIROGLYPHICS (Institute for Further Studies, 20,000 A.D. (North Atlantic Books), INVESTIGATIVE POETRY (City Lights), HYMN TO MAPLE SYRUP (P.C.C. Books), and THE CUTTING PROW (Am Here Books). And some of these poems appeared in a few other publications whose names have been lost by the author in these moiling decades.

The publishers thank the Dayton Hudson Foundation for funds from Dayton's and Target stores that aided in the publication of this book. And thanks to our typesetters at Peregrine Publications for their patience.

Coffee House Press books are distributed to bookstores and libraries by our primary distributor: Consortium Book Sales & Distribution, 213 East Fourth Street, Saint Paul, Minnesota 55101. Our books are also available through all major library distributors and jobbers, as well as through the following small press distributors: Bookpeople, Bookslinger, Inland Book Company, Pacific Pipeline and Small Press Distribution. For catalogs and other information, write to Coffee House Press, P.O. Box 10870, Minneapolis, Minnesota 55458.

Library of Congress Cataloging-in-Publication Data

Sanders, Ed.
 Thirsting for peace in a raging century.

 I. Title
PS3569.A49T5 1987   811'.54   87-10237
ISBN 0-918273-25-0 (alk. paper)
ISBN 0-918273-24-2 (pbk. : alk. paper)

TABLE OF CONTENTS

Poem From Jail

POEM FROM JAIL

Montville State Jail
Uncasville, Connecticut
August 8-24, 1961
having attempted to board the
Polaris-missile submarine
the *Ethan Allen*, as a witness for peace

I
Redeem Zion!
Stomp up over
the Mountain!

To live as "beatific
Spirits welded
          together,"
To live with
     a fierce pacifism,
To love in haste,
as a beetle
entering bark,

To dance with
flaming mane,

All these, a man,
I, steaming, proud,
have sought
as a harlot
her jewels & paint,
as belly seeks out
belly;

And we have
demanded that
they ban the bomb,
mouth of death
convulsing upon the earth,
and the bomb gores

the guts of earth
like a split nail
in a foot fetish,
and the salt domes
rumble
as the arse
of a politician,
and Nevada
is a kangaroo
with its pouch
chopped open
by the A.E.C.

And at my ear
was the whirr
of wings,
"red wing,
black wing,
black wing
    shot with crimson,"
and the Bird Flock
stared to my eye,
and always the Birds
flap overhead
    shrieking
    like a "berserk
    tobacco auction":
Pains! Neverbirth! Dieness!

And we have
seen the failure
of Stassen
& the Teller
intervention
& Radford
in there wailing,
also,
for Death.

And Madame

Chiang Kai-shek
too old now
to fuck for the
        China Lobby,

And we have learned
the Hidden History
of the Korean War,
and MacArthur
who retreated
                before
nonexistent
Chinese Hordes,

And we have seen denied
Mao's creation,
And we have denied
van Gogh's Crow
shrieking on the
                horizon,
and Rouault's Jesus.
Chant   Chant
        O American!
lift up the Stele
        anti   bomb;
O American
        is there
an Eagle of Pacifism?
        Is there
a bevy of symbolic
        Birds?

The Rot Bird,
        The Claw Hawk,
The Sexy Dove,
        The Cormorant
            of Oceanus,
The Sea Crow
        of bloody claws,

Pigeon of the dance
　of the belly,

　　　　Birds
　　　　Birds
Shrieks and furry assemblage
　　　　Birds
　　　　Birds
Blurred birds in flight
　　　　Birds
　　　　Birds
da Vinci's tail feathers,
　　Dream of Youth
　　　　Birds
　　　　Birds
Ginsberg's birds Ginsberg's
sacred scroll to Naomi,
Birds of the fluttering eyes,
　　　　　Birds never asleep,
　　　　　diaphanous eyelids.

Between the
Bevy of Birds
& the Sexy Lamb
there is nothing Else.

The Father negative
The Son negative
The Holy Ghost negative.

　　Aphrodite
　　Kallipugos
　　remains, the
hieroglyphs remain,
　　"Trees die
　　but the Dream
　　remains,"
van Gogh & Ginsberg,
The Burning Bush,
The Trembling Flank,

All remain.
Anubis & the
            power of Amulets,
The Beetle of Endlessness,
            they remain.
My flesh abides.
My electrical meat
            chatters for
a wink of eternity
between dark cunt
            and the grave.

II
Trembling   Trembling
murderous flank
of Now,

Napoleon
            is Now
& was
      & shall,
Napoleon
    stomping all
    over Europe; &
Europa has an
older meaning,
        Europa fucked
        for centuries
        by the Bull of Zeus;
        &
        Pasiphaë
        Pasiphaë, also,
        what contortions
        had you
        to writhe thru
        to receive
        the prick
        of the Bull!
        you O Pasiphaë
        inside the

sacred cow-skin
of Crete,
as the long tool
of the Bull arched
and gored its way
to your snatch,
O Pasiphaë
what thrill
& thunder
you felt,
& what nutty
offspring,
ah the Karma
of that fuck;

"No man who has spent
a month in the death cells
believes in capital punishment

No man who has spent
a month in the death cells
believes in cages for beasts"

No man.
      fucking in the sheaves,
      leaping in the aether,
      lusting for the sun,
      I, a man, my skull
      lined with bird-roosts,
      a man, disjunctive
      coalescence of thoughts,
      trembly, bristling,
      tense beyond belief,
      wandering, relating
      thing to thing,
      balling the All,

hands twisting in
          Moistness,
heart bubbling in

Vasthood,
eyes boucing to th'
Glaze,
brain pucking in th'
Word-steam,
legs sucked in to
Oceanus.

Anubis grins slyly
at the dock,
O American,
O Traveler.
The Sun boat
enters the Vastness,
Anubis stomps
with the Sun shafts,
& the man awaits,
the sun, the
eye of the
Trembling Lamb.
Move onward
O Traveler
of thick sandals
& matted hair,
flouting your
choice patterns,
for you shall
enter the
Mountain,
& the warmth
of the living
darkness, the
warmth as the warmth
between bellies,
& the closeness
as the closeness
there.
Carve a staff
traveler, carve
it with the days,

notch it with
the ways and paths,
in the journey,
under the corn furrow,
where Persephone
is ravished by
her gloomy lover,
Dis, Pluto,
& Persephone is Darkness
also;

You shall Enter,
Traveler,
   in the myriad
directions of the
         prepositions,

      & bounce in
      & bounce over
The Trembling Flank

      & enter in
      & enter over
The Sexy Lamb
      & shriek in
      & shriek over
The Sun-shafts
         and Sun-barge.

III
And I have crawled
thru the forest
near the Doom's Day machine,
puking blood
& clutching guts,
And I have clutched
my Amulet, Ammonite,
for dreams,
& have used
my sacred slab

of Voidal Concretions
as pillow
& have clutched
my scrolls,
& have held
the covenant of my mind
and certain artifacts,
as sacred,
and have notched
my staff with
the times,
& have clothed
the body with
feathers from
the Bevy of Birds,
& my arms thrust
themselves out
of feathers,
prick dangles
out of feathers,
head barfs itself
out of feathers;
on my feet are
sandals,
in my heart
is a ravenous Duck;
& I have laid bare
my choice patterns,
freaked in the
shit of Being,
& I am laid
bare in the
     Burning Bush,
& have pissed
out of the holly leaves,
& I am innocent
& my whiteness
is as the
whiteness of the Lamb.

And we have
seen the men
farting around
in Geneva,
and the governments
have not clasped
one another
as lovers,
shedding the
buffer zones,
confronting
each other
in Nakedness.

No, they have
not halted hate.
Yes, it is true;
Death shall assume
the continuum.
If I am turned
to atomic death
here in my cell,
Let me leave behind
for earthologists
a masturbation,
poetry on
toilet tissue,
love-body of
continuing
nonviolence;
and I shall
project myself
to that time
where I am
clad in feathers,
& my mind
is ejaculated
into the Cosmos,
& I breathe
the god-breath,

& dance
in the rays
of Nonviolence,
staring into forever.

IV
Whom
do we blame
as we stomp
upstage   downstage
left center
                right center
beaming
        in the wings,
balling
            in the orchestra;
Whom do we
blame, O Traveler,
in your journey
thru the
thighs of Cosmos,

        O Traveler
let us blame
the cowardly,
& those in charge
of money,
the economists
& the profiteers,
& the hidden
men in the
military,
& all those who
profit by Death,

And let us place blame
upon
"the enormous
organized cowardice."

O Zeus
may I come forth
bearing a vase & cakes
in the presence
of the gods

may I walk
by the side of my lake
every day
without ceasing

& may I stand
in a perpetual tremble
near the rock pool

and may the waters
bear back
a reflection
          in godhead

may pierce my face
into the way
of darkness

may I receive offerings
in the underworld
with the flowers
crescent
on the dock
of Lethe

may I build then
my tomb
& may I go out
in triumph,
O Zeus
Great-grandson
of the earth,
O Zeus,
third generation

from Chaos,
O Zeus,
grandnephew
of the
Spectres of Vengeance!

Morphelized
motherfucking
        bad-faithed
puke-lips of a
hesitant puker!
Puke dropping to
a bottomless pit!
sore of a thousand
pustules!
mammary
spitting out
clabber!
matriarchal
desensitized demon
vaunting
antilove!
septic excrescence
cut in lozenges!
Endless flypaper,
barrier between
bellies,
hater &
desensitizer
that lies down
between
the bride
        and bridegroom,
Paper cup that
expands to
an incredible
Vastness!
Steel that slits
the throat of
the Sexual Lamb,

Buttocks
with a painted face
and a tongue sticking
out the asshole!

. . . . . . O Jesus!
am I howling
at my country again,
America of the
United States,
where the
new Now culture
is balling its
way toward
the pluperfection.
America which
is th'only
choice left
and place
for the great
      Goof City.

V
Do, nipple
of wet nurse,
cascade,
in chant time,
cascade,
voice behind
the Waterfall
    of Whiteness,
nipple that
dropped on me,
moist &
budded, beautiful,
full & yielding,
nipple,
butterfly
on a white mountain,
and the body
behind breast

rocking,
and the voice
behind breast
singing,
and the warmth
there
beyond belief;
cascade,
nipple bursting
out of brightness;
and the cunning
be there, also,
of the wet nurse
as she played
with me,
there in the
half-light,
and the breast
lowered
from above,
and she bubbled
the milk
on to her hand
and I licked
from there
which I shall
never
forget,
& shall never cease
from sensing;
wet nurse
unhooking brassiere,
then brassiere
in disarray
& breasts
dropping from under
the whiteness of cloth;
Vastness dangling
         in Vastness,
light

cascading
among shadows;
breasts laid softly,
touching
cheek and eye,
eye never to forget,
never,
though the memory
be tattered
and the mind
be shredded.

VI
Goof City,
Infinite cock
& granite snatch,
& whiteness
as almond
out of the husk,
& strange sounds
     There,

temple of
Aphrodite
Kallipugos,

O City
"whose Terraces
are the color
of stars,"

your monuments
the reflection
of crystal,

O City,
thou art beautiful
as the rubies
in thy women's
navels,

thou art as
carefully painted
as thy dancers,

The blueness of
your water
is as a
tinted eyelid,

you are a
nipple
on a mountain,

your streets
are as cross-cords
over belly flesh,

your gates
are as parted lips;

Goof City,
where every choice
is allowed,
        Goof City,
the city of the
Trembling Flank,

Smile & Crotch
without fester,

City without
the Great Cancer

& Cancer not
worshipped
on its Altars,

nor bloated motion,

Goof City,
laughter
laughter
and flaming Teeth.

VII

"The Doomsday Machine. A Doomsday Weapon System might hypo-
thetically be described as follows: Let us assume that for ten billion
dollars one could build a device whose function is to destroy the earth.
This device is protected from enemy action (perhaps by being situated
thousands of feet underground) and then connected to a computer, in
turn connected to thousands of sensory devices all over the United States.
The computer would be programed so that if, say, five nuclear bombs
exploded over the United States, the device would be triggered and the
earth destroyed."   — Herman Kahn

And the "Case"
for disarmament
was read &
chewed up
in the mind.
And as I
sped by
I wanted to
explain,
the Birds I found
in, on, around,
myself
when I looked, &
the Theory of Anubis,
The Trembling Flank,
The Sexual Lamb,
The Amulet of Ammonite,
The Beetle,
All these,
as I sped past
and spent the life
perfecting
Orgasm.
Yes, I

was a fuck-
ing Unilateralist
& was
stalking among th'
Machinery
& stood at
the closure
where the
Doom's Day Box
sucks in its data
from the air
and was a
stave of flesh
among reeds of metal,
and the voice,
the mind's lance
out of the mouth,
blended with metal noise,
as a trill commixed
in the tinkle
of reeds;
and I loved
to walk in Machinery
& stroke the
Antennae
pronged out of
the soil,
& mix my voice
in the din There:
Hate is a murrain!

Krrrr
from the Machine

Fuck off, Death Machine!

Krrrrtelinnnnq
from the Doom box

Death Metal!!

Krrrrrrrrr,

and I
was coughing Thoreau
at them
in my
Civil
Disobedience
in that forest
where the
Doom's Day Machine
lay buried,
projecting its
death Antennae
in the air;
& I walked
and wailed
The Machine
be placed
under U.N. control;
& remained there,
wailing,
till they programed
the Doom's Day Box
against
Trespassers;
And it came to pass
that each pacifist foot
in the hallowed
enclosure
was a trigger,
And I
consulted
the magic
to create an
implosion
of Love
to balance th'
explosion

of Hate
there.

But all I made
was a mild
Aphrodisiac
& set loose
some platonic vapors;

And then stood
in the Forest,
howling by megaphone
at the Closure,
and they pro-
gramed the Doom's
Day Machine
against picketing
also,
& the Moan
of the epilept
passed my teeth,
& my Eye
before the claws
of the Rot Bird
was as a dead horse
under a vulture,
and my Eye
was dancing
freak beams
on itself,
& my mind
was as a feed-bowl
in the flash
of bird claws,
& I strode
to the desert,
& walked the roads,
& fell to a
crawl,
onward,

bloody glaze
bloody tongue
bloody hands.

VIII
to
flip was to flip
like the Spiral
Galaxy,
Brain slain in the
word-stream,
& the arms
were crooked up
to ward off Void,
and my heart
was as a bird
buffed up
to a wall
in the wind;

The road
twisted
like a knife
across the desert
& slashed
        the throat
of Mountains,
& I crawled,
onward,
clutching guts
and coughing blood,
scrawling poems
on rocks
with a charred log
& laughing
to watch
a desert burst
wash out
the lines;
and crawled

all onward,
& entered the
Mountain,
Yes! crawled in
to the vastness,
crawled in
to squirm it out
with the
Grand Machine!
the lights descend
into the Darkness;
Demeter is roused
                out
by my Entrance,
& the ravening Lovers,
Dis and Persephone,
scream Darkness;
lamp-glares
float in the Black;
Brightness
is thrown back
as a glare
from beads
        of sweat.

IX
Overflow
from an end-
less bedpan,
Mind oozing to
the outerstice,
& I have Entered,
eruptum spiritus,
downward, by
the shriekway,
downward;
& the man, me,
stomped into the
flip-stream; and th'
tears, outpukes,

inflips, cellular rot,
the eyes eyes balling
in the flip-stream
ears ears sucking
in the Vasthood
mind mind in the
Tremble drama
heart heart merely
a relay station
brain brain slain
over Goof City;
these are the words
and this
is the man,
Mind behaving
like a berserk
foot fetish,
brain valves torn
in the word stream,
brain balling
the outerstice;

The Milky Way is a meeting of Maenad
Floodlight stagger
the sunflower,
Flowers jerk off
in infinity;

Bristling in the
bat black,
mind spews out
to Nebulae;
   balling the All;
Darkness; swiveled
   into the Mountain;
Shriek it All!!
   Wand waved
over the thigh!
Sucked to the
Vortex,

Universal Hole,
Vastness,
clutching my Amulet,
Ammonite for dreams;
I spew
down thru the
mountain,
gone, flipped to
the reservoir,
dark lone
into the dark
to stomp it out
with the Metal Queen.

Moon wraps its legs around the earth,
Birds perch on a trellis of air,
Eye is the Rot Bird,
Heart is the Claw Hawk,
Crotch is in the Pelican.

CEMETERY HILL

Mollie Cravens Sanders
1903-1957

CEMETERY HILL

The scene: March 7, 1957—Cemetery Hill, at the foot of which we lived—11:00 P.M., death of mother—mother appears in my room, calls name, touches, then floats out to Death Barge—late-night vision of the Death Barge floating thru the sky & entering the dawn sun disc.

And the hands
with white veins
There
dropped on me
from above
and
boiling boiling boiling
the breath of fire
came boiling
and the white eyes
floated out upon
the darkness
in my room
& the voice
called out from There
my name;
11:00 P.M., March 7,
1957: silence,
and floating up over
the hill
beyond the Cemetery
was Apparition
with veins full
of white blood
& white eyes
beaming
berserkness,
Nameless,
a Phantom,
never to enter again
the house she curst

& to have grown thin

in the curse house
down from the
Cemetery Hill
where I knew
Death would
enter early
after my
Grandmother
had
misinformed
me about
Death:
"you shall
nevah die."
& my mother
hipping me later
bout Death
& I ran
out onto the terrace
and faced the Cemetery
up on the Hill
where the winter
sunrise glistened
off the nameplates
There,
Death-rays
focused into
young-eye;
yes I ran
out on to Terrace
in a death-vulsion,
for Grandmother
had said that
Drs. would
make me live
forever,
& I cried there,
stomped into the
Death-chain,
which I had

fled, age 5,
fled fled;
& always
the sun-shafts
glittering off of
tombstones
on the hill
above
my home
meant Death;
Death was
a hill with
tombstones for
teeth,
a Grandmother,
a mother
without hope,
and in the
mornings
a rain crow
exuding Death
in the trees;
And day now
puking itself
up over the
Horizon
reflects
on Cemetery
Hill,
beams upon
the ground
where my mother
lies in a beige suit
in a dark brown
coffin,
Ears laden
with earrings,
& a necklace
on the neck;
and on the

night she died
I saw the
Barge of Death
float out into the Black
& the death ship
full of cakes & vases
entered the Plexus,
freaked itself
in the sun's eye;
& I heard her voice
at 11:00 P.M.
silence: March 7, 1957
and she floated
up over the Hill
beyond the Cemetery
& entered the
Sun barge
& when
dawn
was balling
the Hill
she was
sucked into
the Sun.
.

.
O I have
seen seen seen!
her floating
in the Barge
& she was
as a sunflower
invaded by floodlights,
& her eyes
were white
& her veins
were full
of white blood
and her
mind opened out

& the brain valves
were turned open
and she entered
the Brilliance,
& her mind
was staggered
in the flood
of phenomena;
and I have heard
oh I have heard
my mother
on the barge
of death,
seduced into the rainbow,
led into the current,
an Eye flinging freak-beams
on itself,
a telephone book smeared
with blood;
and I have heard my mother
as her shade stomped out
of the steaming flesh,
and her voice claws
out of the night there,
whose hands were
so beautiful,
whose hands
hooked out at the
oxygen tent
as she lay dying,
puked into the death rattle
bones arattle,
katakakic stomp-out
of the Blossom!
Frenzy of the
Time Murrain!
Death Meat cooling off!
Sunflower out of the flesh!
All out   all out!
.

.

And then she
went out upon
the Trembling Flank
and went forth upon
the Great Necklace of Energy
& rode out
in the
Death Barge
and entered where
the Scarab
dangled from the Neckstrands
,
and the brain
talked freely,
& she then stood
in a perpetual
tremble
on the Black Back
of the Scarab
and she was caught up
in the whirr of wings
There,
& she became full
in the great
Plasm of Being,
& her Eye-Heart-Mind
went berserk in the
desire and fulfillment.
.

.

Eyebrow
in the time-blossom
Ear swiveled in
to th'Nipple,
drool drr
ripping
in the Cascade,
brow into
Breast Gulf

& her mind
entered
the Vastness
& the Cosmos
quaked,
& her Eye
entered upon
itself
in deliverance,
&
forever into
tremble and nothing,
always into
tremble and nothing,
Last Breath
into
tremble and nothing,
Spiritus Aeterna
into
tremble and nothing,
Crotch entering
into the
Word-machine,
Eyelash
dragged over
the time-stream,
ejaculata
in cosmo,
the Dark
enters
& reenters
the flesh
& the
Vagina
comes into being
around the
endless Phallus,
& the heart
appears
beyond the Eye

& forever
verberates
in the time-plex,
and
she enters
in continuing
desire
with the
Angelloi,
tense & bristling
on the terrace
of stars;
& "word-lines"
were crushed
in the
Vibrata
& were
to the ear
as resin
in a
foot fetish,
and Hello
out there!
cry of the
Shade
& she was
caught up
in the
utter Roar,
Plexus now,
no more
in the Vortex
but
became
the Vortex,
became the
Lamb &
the blood
flowing
out of Lamb.

November 5, 1961

ARISE GARLAND FLAME

Arise! out of me garland flame!
Arise Arise rose wraith
out of my billion back-brain cells
I come I wandering
down to your biered womanness
in your green untombstoned grave
up over the hill
I shall write 4 poems to you
from 4 directions
in my pilgrimage
from the West up Cemetery Hill
from the East along the ridge
from the South up the long slope
from the North along the row of trees and
over the fences

Arise wraith in me
that is of thee
come forth gentle spirit from out my heart
through the power of these
my imperatives.
Enter my brain with flares searing the meat
light up the animal halls
lain dark through these
phylogenous aeons
I shall be your mystes
to paint my flesh &
char my embers in the service
of your gleaming fane
O woman of the Disk
come forth come forth come forth
screaming genius! come forth
I am the meat-chain
born of your legs spread
over the linen
falling in a proskynetical glory
to munch thy toes dangling
out of a slatted boat

in the dawn:
Blaze up in me hierogyne
that I may examine myself
whom you made whom you
rolled from your legs
in the service of Replication
Blaze up with your eyes painted
the myriad arms of the DISK to
lift you finally
up from the showered halo
dawn sun over the protestant stones
Death Boat stroked by the Arms
fingers slid along brow
to touch the Eye
blinked
open in the Boat
mouth free to pucker or smile
hands heating the forehead long lain electrically still

all all all hands all moving
all from the sun disk all from the boat
all in the radial fingers
all from your rising, Mollie,
burn, rise in me your son,

come forth!
wet woman bathing
breast poked with
a lonely finger
shoulder & back
washed by the
tiny hands
to know her
bush fragrant
with soap

breasts dangling
over the hairy heads
You, Robert & I
wet children
from your crotch
under the faucet,
The memory gleams!
plates of armor
fall from my psyche
the water scalds
with our love

with our love
We are one
line of replication,
the meat-chain
spurts from the legs,
We are the
first slimy thing that
bubbled out of a warm
water spring
in the kryptozoic aeon,
the line of
evolution hangs
from the prostate,

Arise wet woman Mollie mother
bathed & beautiful
free from the strangle of
the slick, scented satin rubbed
over your face & the
ruffles pressed down on your nostrils.
Bloom, flare, blink open
or come at least to
my mind, o memory,
where the flares are set
to light up
at your footfall

June-August 1964

THE PILGRIMAGE

There is nothing on the
wet morning grass
not even a mound
to mark the grave.
I have started in the
shade of the walnut
trees & walked
up the hill
to make my
proskynesis at thy altar
O daughter of Ra
how elaborately the morning kisses
this hill with its teeth
I faint under the
magic rays of the sun
which devour the ground.
Just to the south
by the wilted flowers
of a grave newly sodded
the rain has forced
a hole that goes
deep down down down to the only Acheron
first finger then stick
I poke to find its end
THERE IS NO END
no tears Ed
worship her with
the flowers you brought
build her a monument of flowers
prothesis of words
in the only adoratio possible.
When I wake I find
the flowers fallen
in the shape
of an arm & a hand!
a flower-glyph on the grave lawn!

The hand lies westward
& the arm of flowers points
from the East
where Barque of the Morn
floats forth
with bundles of sun-arms
for Ra's benefaction
with benevolent arms of light
hands out of the disc
peace fingers groping
all the transeminentia
—gathered together—
swathed in Ra

The Arms Arms of Ra
dipping in benemagnificence
hook hands cusping in gentleness
smooth arms from the disc
over the cemetery
the rain crow at peace now
storm over, wet dew, hot sun
only the wet grave newly sodded
drawing my Eye down
to Acheron Acheron of All
at the end of the rain tube
under the brown bronze lid
& above the satin
Acheron Acheron Acheron

July 1964

PRAYER FOR THE UNITY OF THE EYE

pale hands,
sucked of genius,
stroke my forehead
in dark.
Rub the ridges
over the eyes,
hands,
that the ache
end.
cheek stroked,
nose entered
by pearly finger,
bring all
the shards
of my eye home,
hands.

her hand touches the
right of the eye ⊃

her knuckle blesses
the sinister: ⊲

the eye ball is brought
home through
gentle finger prayers
⊂⊙⊃

the eyelash is
made
          lux   urious
          ⊂⊙⊃

& the lines of
fulfillment
are fashioned
in the
rotunda of her
clenching hands

PINDAR'S REVENGE

Ἄριστον μὲν ὕδωρ
— PINDAR

I know that the sun rising
is a temporary thing,
that the sun obtuse on clouds
at 30 thousand feet from the
airline windows is an
equal particle, that
Ra is a shard, an
ostracon from a forbidden
cycle of the aeons.
Nor god nor pulsing phantom forever
but that I live at the mansion of earth
for eighty years in the warmth,
the children off to space,
the chickens still crowing
at sunup, but our
hearts beat lugubrium lugubrium lugubrium
at Ra's pink-fingered sinking

42 billion years
then zap
then 42
zap
we are caught

The meat-chain
born of
the prostate,
born of the
cusping egg —
caught, ended,
slashed. We are
led by the calf
to the thin
arroyo

to be slaughtered in droves
driven into the eyes and
slashings of the manglers,
that little drama,
no matter,

42
zap
"we are now
in the
electromagnetic
cycle"

IT lives.
Enormous breathings
& compressions
of IT

                    July 24, 1965
                    Returning to New York, 30,000
                    feet, from the Berkeley Poetry
                    Conference. The quote and
                    the concept of the 42 billion-
                    year zap, are from Olson,
                    from the Berkeley lectures.

DREAMS OF SEXUAL PERFECTION

SHEEP-FUCK POEM

The ba ba lanolin fur-ears

        sex
      Trembling Lamb
where I enter the
        matted meat
of the trembly sheep
the cunt warm
      & woman-sized
offered by the lamb
which is surely the
lamb of god, the
lamb of the Trembling Flank
& the bucking & sighing
when the prick sputs
the hot come
        into loins
& the lamb looks back
with her eye
     & glazes me
in the freak-beams
& we are oily & atremble
    in the lanolin glaze
      frenzy morning field
       hay hidden
        fuck-lamb
      day in bloom torrent.

              November 1961
              February 1962

THIS IS THE PRAYER WHEEL & VISION

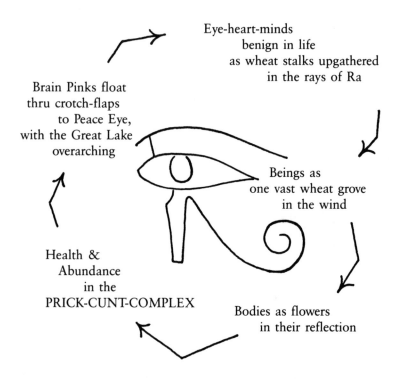

Eye-heart-minds
benign in life
as wheat stalks upgathered
in the rays of Ra

Brain Pinks float
thru crotch-flaps
to Peace Eye,
with the Great Lake
overarching

Beings as
one vast wheat grove
in the wind

Health &
Abundance
in the
PRICK-CUNT-COMPLEX

Bodies as flowers
in their reflection

ELM-FUCK POEM

in to the oily crotch
        place dick

go up
    kiss the gray-white tree
fondle the crotch
        sweet juice there flowing

        to which you place the tongue
        to suck the pulse of the

            Hamadryad

        come into the cool gray
    bark the hair-gray color of Persephone

            how difficult it is
            to be fucked
            in the volcano!

        ahhhhh but how sweet
        the elm tree's rheuming
        gray bark made black
        by the viscid
        fluid flowing

    out of the branches—

            I place my dick
    in the tight in-fold of the elm V
        —heat of the summer—

        fuck till the come drift
        down thru the bark furrows
        fuck thru the warm afternoon
        sperm steams in the sun

birds in the branches
sun shines thru
seed steam
thru
wing of butterfly
wetting its
furry fluttering tips

I have given myself to the elm
I have soaked the dryad's shawl
What a wonderful world,
a palace of gentle sexual aggression.

Tree baby!
how I love to rim
your bark slits
kiss the leaves
above your dripping
elm crotch oozing
at the base

I place my penis
over the mish

& slowly start to
shove it deeper
encasing it in to deep deep elm snatch

Let me sing

of a need to fuck
at once the tousled leaf elm
place the lingam
in wet tree oil—
slowly O lovely lady,
such care & kindness
—as when rabbit nose
snoozles a carrot—
but give it thrill jabs,
give it to her,

worship the Dryad
fill her with foaming

under the elm boughs
heavy in the summer wind

to fill all holes,

lovely longing lone lingam
plugging the vastness.

Do you feel it, pretty humans,
& do you know

a tree-twat is as good as
a buttock
& the elm branch is the dryad's breast.

1966

HOLY WAS DEMETER
WALKING TH'CORN FURROW

It was impossible for one to read C. Kerényi's *Eleusis* and George Mylonas's *Eleusis and the Eleusinian Mysteries* without falling in love with Demeter. In 1967, this love was combined with a long-visioned *idea* of making love with the Earth: that is, the visionary embodiment of the Egyptian sem-ta 𓋴𓏏𓂝

i.e., earth fuck. Such a possibility, as felt in early 1967, triggered off a hunger for instant Elysium. The vision was of a plowed field, springtime, bright sunlight, and Demeter, her arms full laden with corn sheaves, approaches the angst-eyed earthling Edward Sanders, in April 1967, as a personal *Be-in* that raised the earthling's mind for all his life to the Permanent Nodule. The first version of this poem was prepared for a reading with Ted Berrigan at Israel Young's Folklore Center on September 5, 1967.

Fucked the corn-meat
sprouted of the river
in the fetish of the lob.

Sucked off the corn clits
curly and cute
in the earth squack

spurt strands swirling
the soil

    When Deo walked down
    the dusty spring road
    I nearly fell afaint

    I tried to
    tell her "I am
    no Poseidon"

    but she smiled
    & said this: "O earthling
    even a poet

as thou art,
and a punkly one,
can be a thrill
to the λουσία

for I have been
washed in the River!
And all are good!
And oh how I shall love thee,
little pale poet of earth!"

Not a word more mouthing
Demeter,
pale as husk fibres,
shy as new corn
        near to the
            husk tip

bent over the furrow
with blessings,
by the flesh-plowed river bank

Total Beauty in the odors
of new sprouted dirt.

Bent over   Bent down
& I flipped it to the
buns, and knew the
god-rose in the snatch
felt the god-butt
knew her &
spurted thru the
blessings, droplets
of spangled jissom
in the Red Halls of
Demeter, the Goddess.
Pumped in the berry bushes

to know her, suck off
the wine berries
smeared on her buttocks,
ate Demeter, corngirl,
out of her salinity

ahhh ahhh ahhh

Demeter   pale as husk-fibres
shy as new corn
        near to the
                husk tip

Total Beauty in the odors
of new sprouted dirt.

A mocha milk shake
is not so sweet
as your buns
pouring out
    the godly

        bun sqush

And then Demeter
turned around
and sank to her
knees   knee caps sink
out of sight
in the plow clods,
white goddess-palms
reach up
rub my knees
& then to suck
my poor pale
earthling prong—

see her crouched there
(the vision, forever in mind, of)
husk fibres hanging out of ass
white new corn

is as white as her
lip-padded chomp teeth
O-ing my pole.

And later
a flash spread
in loam dirt

leg of the Deo to th'south-southeast
leg of the Deo crookt up
                to th'south-southwest

the back of her snug
in a pure 'n' perfect
north-south furrow

I shall kiss the fibres
shall buss th'
o'erlaid soil with
wan lips & desirable

freckles of your
belly as Indian
corn in an
autumn bundle.

Torrid was th'goddess groin
tongue moth frying
in the
candle of the earth-clit

And maybe you think
that when dark Deo came
that it was not
a different experience—

One wd have thought
that the gods were rerunning
the submergence of Atlantis

so much did
the plow plot
quake around us
     as my poet's tongue
flash-flitted my Deo
     10,000 times

till grope quake
seized her crotch's
     pink lick-node

"ahh, sweet
poet of earth," she cried,

"oh sing to me

sing to me."

& the pale beams of the
Cosmic Intrusion
          enter

the brain —

glorious Da-Mater
walking away —

oh watch her walk away!

dripping my come over
corn leaf, back
to her bower among the deathless,

burnished buttocks etching the Sky—
honed of a finer tool than ever
carved a grope grape—rose
leaves not as interesting as
the wrinkles of her ass
ahh for another pinch
of skuz from thy
omphalic glory*
my lady of the corn.

ahh what a thrill is a god grope

*Note: thou scoffest, no doubt, and mutter that I am as insolent as
Ovid, when I suggest that one might have a relic of Demeter's
omphalic corn lint. Indeed, the tense is now in the pluperfect, for we
smoked it in a waterpipe, Robert Bly & I, in Ann Arbor, Michigan,
one afternoon in 1969, on a Resist Poetry Tour.

BY HONOR, BY AGONY

by honor

by agony

by the Cretan horns
by the altar
of Breasts

by the soaking of the
Dryad's shawl

& the cool vagina
hanging from the Elm.

Eat of the Acorn's navel
& suck the sugar of
the Earthworm's logic

1967

ADIOS DIAMOND SUTRA

THE V. F.W. CRAWLING CONTEST

Wet smells above
the
counters of pine,

stock tanks full of Pabst,
end of the May Day picnic,
unpainted 1 by 12's

spanked by the
slaps of raw hands
selling.

Kshshsplipt! kshshsplipt!
& o'er & o'er
the tabs were pulled
in the spring breeze

as the endomorphs massed
together in a groveling huddle
to begin the V.F.W. Crawling Contest

you should have seen them
25 or 30 humans
packed on hands and knees

some wearing basketball knee pads,
work gloves, chaps,

4 or 5 pairs of jeans
to ward off ouch.

There was the air of festival
one of the crawlers
with a propeller-topped beanie

above his brow

men with their dogs
men of position
appliance stores & rectitude.

At sunset
the first day

they began to yell at me
"Come on, Harry, come on & quit!"

My Levi's were
wasted at the knees
which were raw like
floor burns at a
roller rink

I lay in the
dry weeds   I wadded
my poplin golf jacket up
for a pillow

thought of the moon

There was a screech
of brakes
& a sharp voice:
"Not in here you don't!"

A teenage boy
lurched from the jalopy
and puked on
me—an offal
of white lightning
plus god knows—something
with pasta and marinara sauce.

I am happy.

In the town dump
I saw the local fire freak
stand staring transfixed
drool on chin

    looking at the fire
    of the evening burning
    hands in his raincoat pocket

Quietly I crawled past
not wanting to tempt his Zippo

    For a minute I crawled up upon the
    rusty bedsprings and bounced
    upon my back

        watching the sunset
        smelling the mutant steak sauce
        & burnt tin cans

        mosquitoes mating
        'bove the muck.

    Late that night a highway dept
    tractor nearly
    pulled a tmesis job
    on my lower legs

    crawling up the hill
    along the dreaded edge
    of the interstate fear-via
    sweating like a rodent
    of the ditch

    whooshomm! whooshomm! whooshomm!
    tones dropping on the *sh*

all through the night
rusty monsters roaring past.

Bloody-fingered   bloody-toed
the hours & days & weeks
went by with tedium
clawing through mire
on the way to muck.

I've seen all the muds
red muds — green muds — brown muds —
muds mixed with sand, gray mud, mud
that smelled — God, had I crawled
through a sewer?

There's a lot of
protein hurled to the
roadsides

almost unbroken lines of choff
across the country

random splotches of yum-yum
colophons of beer tabs,
tire hunks, condoms,
havatampa wrappers
and paper cups.

I received
in my oil mitts
the choff.

My hands.

As if I had dipped
them in a vat of rubber
cement —
filth bits spackling the glue.

My posture grew wormy—to wit: I
could only slide along on my stomach
or back, or side,

        & more & more
        I had to rely upon my
        tongue

        a terrible mistake—
        nor Sucrets nor lozenge
        could scrape free
        the gizzardly condition
        of my larynx.

           I blushed
           to gobble the
           bladelets of
           grass, bent w/ grime

but grass was my Alka Seltzer

        after
        a questionable
        roadside gunge-gobble.

Every night
I saw the sunset but
somehow shifted in my sleep to
awaken facing the
dawn—

(a habit which later saved my life)

        I learned to sing
        fearless I yodeled
        shameless shameless
        singing for my soul
        like Mrs. Meyerhoff
        in a 1953
        Christmas pageant,

my sempiternal gravel raga.

I offered prayer
to God, praised be.

O Theos,
enter my gnarled cracked
knuckles & penitent mind
I am a cur most foul, I
am wax
O Butterfly

O Deus

Help me to scoot
along under Thy
temporary grace before
Thou shalt
crunch me beneath
Thy purple sandals

Help those in pain
Help me,

Help Thy ghosts assemble

Help the Perfections
reappear

Help!

Somehow I reached
a long downgrade
phew!

The top of my head
bashed a plank
shouldn't have closed my eyes
hooked the edge of my skull
up over the board's edge
so that the splintery edge

of the board fit in with the
groove of my left temple

ouch.

I lay then on my back
flopping on top of the board
wet sausage on a spoon

and then as if it were
a surf board in a down-slide
of water gravel

I scooted down, inch by inch,
pushing off with my toes and feet—

       I began to get the beat
       in my Irish soprano
       hummed old Beach Boys singles
       I got the beat
       music throbbed in the stomped dust
       puffing around my eyes.

       On my back it
       would take me
       sometimes
       5-10 minutes to
       crawl past

a dead animal —
how humiliating
when a line of ants

would abandon
the flattened possum
& try to take me.

As I approached the
drive-in restaurant

saliva began to drip from
my crust-cambered lips

No automobiles parked
silently full of potato-eating
families
    did leave the lot
    as I rounded
    the bend
    out of a clump of
    ditch weeds

when just like a performer
onto a stage
my head appeared
in the bright lights

first just my noggin
on the oily plank

then the beauteous vista
of my fragrant bod

staring up
at the white-framed
screen of the order window

"a hot dog
   & baked beans please
      just drop it in the tar."

Some humans
would try to
look casual

when the
saucers land

The Sears-mod
taurus neck in
white bells
driving a supercharged Mustang 350

parked
stepped over me
ordered

a banana malt
plus *pommes frites*
looking good looking cool.

I herped away
with my
wiener & beans
to suffer luncheon within
a nearby concrete culvert

& vom, vom, vom, vom
the rain began, I
crawled from the culvert
into the vomorama,
filth to lave—

a typical drop would strike my stomach
wattled like a streaked muck meatloaf

to curdle and scour
a speck of dust

which later drops
would bear away.

The waters rose.
I propped my head
upon an old
pile of what appeared
to be a wadded-up overcoat
all stuck together &

glued with last summer's
cobwebs.

Popsicle sticks zoomed past
like narrow rafts
shooting some western rapids.

The storm was not without its
tragedies
    as, snuffed by the sky,
    mice and weak birds
    puked past in the sewery spew.

        An act of the storm
        caused me
                to roll
                down into the
                ditch
                full of water

            past 3-foot boulders
            of happiness

        My head slid first
        into the rivulet
        which was surprisingly deep

        then, like a fallen rafter
        the rest of me plopped
        into the smush.

        I lay still
        as the water swirled
        over the top of my
        sunken head.

                Some sort of branch
                swept
                        down the

creek
during my subsurface revery
& lodged above
me so that
my head was pressed
down and trapped —

talk about panic

My left arm
flailed like a maniac's
My right arm wedged itself beneath
in the rocky sludge.

I rolled a quarter-turn
trying to push
my head up through
the washed-out elm.

The answer — alas —
was a muck dredge
with my face

I turned full face down
lifted my buttocks
scrunched my knees forward

then, like an orator
begging for votes

I began to burrow
with my mouth
in the ditch-bed

ptooey-ing gobs of mud
out of the way —
mud-gobs bubbling down the sluice
in the current

After about 10 frenzied
oral dredge-scoops
I freed my head

    & rolled to safety
    many minutes of barf-spits
    to clean my mouth.

The
rain stopped
buzz-saw bronchitis
began to utter itself in the night

and all was ZZZZ's.

As my good friend
Morpheus began
to throw me out of heaven

I opened my right eye first
to grant it the grace of light

& there it was:

    the boot,
    the heel of which
    was grinding my nose

    grinding left
    grinding right
    in a black V
    of ouch

"Up against the wall, crippled punk!"
hissed a voice
from above the boots.

I obliged
rolling over a few feet

to flatten my
self supine in keening obeisance against a
shed—observing a service of
soft whimpers at the wet foundation
of which

"OK, let's see some identification!"

I fumbled for my
credit cards—begging
for forgiveness

while gum boots
debated aloud
with harumphs and groans
wh'er or not to run me in

but never so sonorous a whine
did win over
the heart of a policeman
as the tale of the V.F.W. Crawling Contest

Ha ha spinach ears.

She visited each afternoon
during that wonderful 100-mile stretch
in the lower foothills

I'd scoot till
we came to a croft
by the side

then head inland
50 feet or so

say grove of locust
say grove of willow trees

She didn't take notes
or bear a recorder

so maybe she wasn't a writer

Together we'd sip a Coca-Cola
she brought me some of those
bend-around plastic straws

The day before we met
I passed a football field
whose garbarge heap contained
a teeming mound of gauze, adhesive
tape and rubber pads   that'd
covered the damaged knees and arms and feet
for the big game Saturday past.

　　　　I just crawled
　　　　into the midst of it
　　　　& somehow the bulk of it
　　　　congealed around me, as
　　　　onward I crawled
　　　　a mummy of gauze.

　　　Joy
　　　whelmed my
　　　eyes as, knee-
　　　caps in gravel,
　　　she slid toward
　　　me, showing herself
　　　spread in a
　　　tattersall dress—
　　　climbing atop
　　　me, leaning above, groins
　　　clinking in
　　　sunshine the
　　　sunshade of
　　　her shoulders
　　　on my face.

Kisses, portable radio, talking,
　　　　for 30 days—

then, poof.

I was not man
enough to get
up to follow
her — &
she was not about to
crawl. She
vanished with no excuse
& on I crawled
out of her range
in the winter heights.

Th'slitherous rocks
sorely did render
my lower hocks
into dog food

    birds flocked
    in a Jungian horde
      to peck up
      the
      hock-hunks

      deserta

So at a
    smashed mailbox
    sundered in the dirt
    a booger-clod of loam
    still aclinging to its
    4-by-4 post painted white

    I paused,

bludgeoned the box
from the post.
I am happy.

I bent it
beat it into the
shape of
a gravy plate
then lay upon it.

To keep it from slipping away
I tied a ditch-sucked
dog leash
        from each side
        of the flattened
        container
        & looped the rope around my neck &
        thus I could slither painless
        face-down elegant fop-flop.

Very cold
I woke up
        45 min.
        before dawn
        face attacked by muskrat.

The little punk
was choffing
hunks out of my frozen cheek

rat cage in Orwell:

        tug on a piece of
        it—pulled it out like
        a snail, and scratching around it
        as if to dig a moat

                ouch. I
wadded up my body, then
drop-kicked
the gnawing little beast

went growling away
just as Dawn began to

lean with rubicund bosom above
the fir-topped hills.

Tears met the dripping.
I crept into the doctor's office
to beg for penicillin.

It took me days of useless pus-crawl
to reach him.
I counted them

3 days
15,000
drips.

It must have been
that prophylactic
I slithered across
last week in Axel's Corner

quite a thrill
hot dusty tum-tum
upon a rheumy gray
balloon.

A maintenance vehicle
finally got me—scrunch!—in the legs,

a snapping sound, then
motor fading distant.

No arteries broken, however, but
it was like crawling with fishhooks
in the legs.

And like a
drunken poet
mumbling in a moment of weakness,
"On to Stockholm / On to Stockholm!"

the void did heal my legs.
I prayed to The Lake.

O Lake of Shooting Stars, the eye-souls
zzzt! zzzt! fall to
fulfillment beneath thy surface.

Merely to touch Thee

Lake

to walk in Thy surf froth
blown by holy winds

this is my prayer.
O Heavenly Lake

just to rest
within the merest
lattice of sunbeams

touching You, somehow saved.

I began to collect
metal items which
I attached to my body with twine

pipes, hubcaps,
lunch pails, hinges, hasps,

40 or 50
pieces of metal
dragging behind me

some of my
metals
I dragged on lines
as far as 50 feet away.

All excited I
entered the forest
flailing arms, pieces of metal
flopping in abandon
scraping and shoving with my
lower stubs

 I looked back
 staring o'er my forehead
 looked at the long

   forested slope
   into the high country

   the crags and secret gorges

   thousands of feet above
   and miles away!

   I crawled
   I groveled
   I conquered.

A FLOWER FROM
ROBERT KENNEDY'S GRAVE

During demonstrations at Nixon's second inauguration, we
watched his limo pass, on the way to the White House; then I drove
over to Arlington Cemetery

January 20, 1973

After
a winding walk
up past the white stones
of snuff,

past the guardhouse
circling circling
around the Catholic henge
to John Kennedy's bright taper
burning on the ground
in windy cold winter after-speech
afternoon

then walk down
to the left-hand

edge of the hill-
ock—there in speechless serenity,

built onto the steepness
a small
elegant
perfectly proportioned
white cross 'bove
white flat marble marker

Robert Francis Kennedy

nearby a fount jets horizontal
over a slab o' stone

water curving down abruptly on the
rock front lip

R.F.K.'s words of race heal
writ upon the rock above
the flat-fount.

Across the walkway
by the grave
a long red rose
with a vial of water
slipped upon the stem end
& wrapped with shiny tape
lay singly
& to the left of it a
basket of yellow chrysanthemums

and this: that
only a whining hour past,
Richard Nixon
oozed down Pennsylvania Avenue
flashing V's from a limousine
behind a stutter-footed wary pack of Marines
their
bayonets stabbing the January
in a thickery of different directions
like small lance hairs
pricked up on the forehead of a
hallucinated drool fiend
during a bummer

but big enough to stab the
throats of hippie rioters

buddy.

I picked a yellow petal

from thy grave
Mr. Robert Kennedy

& brought it home
from Arlington, where many young mourners
stood crying quietly this inauguration day

Picked a dream
          Mr. Robert Kennedy
brought it home in our hearts
burning like a brand in a fennel stalk

Picked a thought-ray
Robert Kennedy

          brought it back from this
          henge of park-side
          eternity

buses of protesters parked
in the lots beneath your hill

          Tears splash
          in the vessels
          of the sun

          Picked yellow
          molecules bunched
          in beauty
          from the beauty fount
          Mr. Robert Kennedy

The peace-ark
glides in the vastness,
though weirdness clings to your death.

But nothing can touch the ark
sails through the trellis of evil
brazen American wrought of light hate

Nothing can touch it
not even pyramidal battlements of gore-spore
nor tricky's pitiless flood
of dungeonoid luciphobian losers.

ADIOS DIAMOND SUTRA

Just a few
days after
the universe

began to implode,
the connoisseur
of mystic rubrics

looked back
as best he could
through the time-gasm

said "Adios
Diamond
Sutra"

THE ICE

A True Tale

It was New Year's
Eve 1959 and there was
no where to make love

They were sitting in the Figaro Café
at MacDougal & Bleecker Streets
sipping an orzata and a grenadine

Bought a small bottle of brandy
went to
Fort Tryon Park
Washington Heights
Columbia Boat Basin

climbed high up in the
rocks   there had been snow

making love
            steep incline between rocks
         tennis shoes gripping
opened his coat and they
wiggled off the rock
and slid down the ice flow

"We're sliding." They couldn't stop
            & the ice thrilled her buttocks

STAND BY MY SIDE, O LORD

So many people have been spoiled Vast Galaxies
It's hard to figure out
where to start

       to study the lives
       of the hieroglyphic
       artists, literally,
       ha

            ha
            how they lived
            what studious
            dumbness they plowed with
            their fingers

for what?   better to follow
a curve
       of mathematics

         curlicues
           of madness
       in a hall of shudders,
       perhaps—

            or was it better
            at the end to
            have followed the
            advice of ancient forefathers?

     Through our technocracy
     & doodling in the genetic spew
     we try to Emanate
     & take our species
     onward into the house
     of the Lord—

     Is that what the message is?

The coronellae
   or th'spaceship helmets
      on the petroglyphs

         are not from space
         but from   the inner eye spray
         of the dumplings
         who stood to try
         to raise
            a whisper
            into the rotting
            gravity of
            soft sadness.

            Grabbst 'ou where I'm coming from,
            muh fuh?

      When she didn't
      like me, I didn't like
               me
      She loved me later,
         & I fell apart.

Now I pray to be whole & gentle
grace-fingers raised up
like wheat
            for the bread of
            the void of paradise.

                  1973

                  —86—

Egyptian Hieroglyphics

A STUDY OF REBELS IN ANCIENT EGYPT

AB-MER
A Love Story of 1985 B.C.

Hathor's farm and school of every art
had a fine broad lake
square as perfection
cornered by the finest acacia trees
the breasts of Isis
hung from the branches

The gardens and orchards of Hathor's House of Life
moiled with abundance, the flocks
of animals grew like the seed of Ptah
under the urging of Hathor

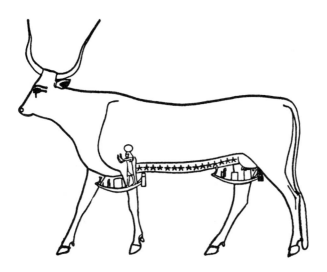

How many hundred weights of honey
lay stored within the House of Hathor,
Countless, the bees of Hathor buzzed within the long reed hives
and poets writing lyrics walked blossom'd acres

So what if the quarter-mile wall
around the House of Hathor was rather in need of repair?
What midget from the
robber camps in the marshes
would climb up over to steal?
What jewels were there to
steal from the House of Hathor?
What thief would want
long poems on parchment?
What could he get for that? since
Limited Signed Editions were thousands of years away.
What was the price of sketches
on old wine casks?
No robber after gold
or red stones would bother
when the graves of the desert
held tons of wealth.

Soldiers patroling the wasteland temples of wealthy dead
with long-snouted dogs on leash
whispered how displeased the vizier's agents were
with Hathor's Rebel House of Life.

By the standards of the time, 1985 B.C.
in the beginning of the first of the
Middle Kingdom dynasties, it was a small House of Life,
but self-sufficient,
collecting to its walls the finest painters, dancers,
singers, poets, musicians, stone workers, wine makers
and tasters of the above, rebels all, full of energy
and full of love of Hathor and Hathor's whispered 'joinder to Ra:
"Part thy robes, O Ra, and we shall conjoin."

Ready were the artists of Hathor to fill the valley Nile
with beatnik potsherds, Hathor lore, papyri drawn with visions
never seen beneath the deity-clogged skies of overarching Nut.

Nothing sang as sweet
as Hathor's singers
No one could raise the skin

and the scatter dance of love
so far into the heights
as Hathor's singers

What a school of singers was the House of Hathor

    None could draw with
    such consummate skill
        as the draughtsmen of Hathor
    No one could raise such thunderous anger
    from petty clerks in the civil government
        as the draughtsmen of Hathor

    and the poets raised up such a complete complex
    of derision and anger:

    "Put trivia upon the basalt blocks. It's
    better than lists of captive slaves" was sort
    of the motto of the House
    which caused the court-creeps rail with anger, urged the
                                                        King
    to snuff out "those uppity scratchers."

What a school of art and verse, the House of Hathor

    Nor could any pluck the harp
    or beat upon a row of drums
    or pick with gentle squalls of notes
    'pon the nefer guitar
    like the women & men there dwelling

What a school of music and drum, the House of Life of Hathor

    Beer was sacred to Hathor
    and every revel
    save that of Apep.

    And ahhh the beer
    produced by the artists
    of Hathor

sweet with dates
the beer grew
within the
barley dough

& the wine dripped lascivious
out of the press
best in the land.

Grumbles and whispers
swept the land con-
cerning the rites of Hathor
held in the House of Life.

All night long they drank
the sacred drool
All night long
the household danced for Hathor
who raised her skirt for angry Ra,
Hathor of the Horns.

The drummers incomparable and
twin-reed flutists urged the swirling,
the dancers shook the sistra
they shook the square tambourines
they clacked the ivory finger-cymbals

& Hathor of the Sycamores
walked toward Ra, and Ra sent
barques of servants underneath
to touch the stars of Hathor.
O rites of Hathor.

Meanwhile
Ammenemes I (1991-1962)
beginning of the 12th dynasty
transferred many artists down the
Nile from the area of Thebes to
Memphis, and notice was served upon
the House of Life of Hathor
to get ready to hit the bricks.

No one at the House of Hathor
wanted to leave sweet Thebes
for Memphis merely to cop
a scope on the "great Art of the
                    past"
just because some jacked-off jackal
of a King desired to push their
minds, therefore their art, therefore
their muscles 4/5/600 years back
to 2600 B.C.

Ab-Mer was an artist lived
at Hathor's House of Life
Ab-Mer the painter/carver

And Ab-Mer was sorely angered
by the Pharaoh.
When he was
        alone
        he shouted
        the King's name

            He threw crocodile dung
            at the sun shouting
            "The worm eat the King!"

            Then, curse upon curse,
            Ab-Mer was fired from
            his job as coffin carver
            at the royal snuff works
            for drawing
            a weirdo version
            of the King's cartouche
            upon a fresh pine box,
            drew an ear
            where the sun disk
            should have been.
            "Son of Ear!" his friends laughed
            in the tented saloon,

"Here's a drink
to getting fired
for the carving
of the King's ear!"

"A fist upon the King!"
"Hathor!" and all drank
and dancing the poets sang.

The sin of the writers, musicians,
dancers, painters, stone workers &
"tasters of combinations" as some
were known who partook of several
skills—the sin in the authorities'
mind was that the House of Hathor
extended all such deific protection
from the kings and queens and
courtoids to all the people,
especially those at the Hathor
House of Life.

"We are the glyphs
we are the people dancing
we are the magic colors
    upon the graven cedar planks
we are the writers we are the
    curls of the melons of the
    gardens
we are the people singing and
    singing on paper
we ARE the ceremonies!"—
this was their attitude.
"The grain belongs to everybody"—
passed about on pot pieces
for those who could read.

When Ab-Mer cursed the Pharaoh,
as common to any police state,
the word drifted up the power
climb adorned with grotesque

additions—the King was
afraid of the curse. What insolent
carver of coffins dared
trash the King!? It will be noted
that the Pharaoh did wear a cobraic
uraeus on a hippie headband 'pon his
mantled brow which was designed
to handle and to ward off the
oncoming vibes of destruction. But,

like kings of all time he never
quite trusted his defenses.
So he put out a contract for the
brickout of Ab-Mer the caustic
carver, with a team of scowling
crude robbers of graves in a
tent town deep in marshes
south in Upper Egypt.

While the goons were floating
down the Nile, Ab-Mer was singing
w/ men and women friends, passing
a paper roll by the cool lake
in the closed court grove on
grounds of the House of Hathor,
upon which roll they all
were composing a satire skit
about the King.

Moans of eager skin
leaked forth till a sword hooked
into the side of the tent
and the rude king's hit men
started to chop, shouting   \
        "Where is Ab-Mer?"
"Ab-Mer, we cut up your face?"—bodies
dashing in the garden
whence Ab-Mer somehow escaped, formulae
of hatred
boiling from his lips.

Late at night Ab-Mer
sneaked back into the compound
to dance with I-mm-eti
the love of his life.

She wore a small stone Ab-Mer painted
with her portrait

as she shook.
He watched her dance, he danced also
and all the sistra shakers, drummers
guitar players surging for Hathor

I-mm-eti dipped back down
upon the dance platform
back bend, shimmy,
back bend

Ab-Mer loved the one who danced
there more than his heart
could bear
        almost.

And when their eyes met
eyes danced out of the sockets
and the eyes took off the eye clothes
and one eye drew atop the other
and the eye tongue slid upon the shiny eye.

Late late the chorus of Hathor sang
as I-mm-eti swayed and shimmied
bounced and leaped into exhaustion.

            But after 15 minutes rest
            the frazzle turned to frenzy
            and torrid need
            o'erwhelmed them.

            I-mm-eti nodded him come to her rooms
            where shards of his drawings ringed the walls

and poems they wrote made love upon the plaster.

And not since Isis taking the form of a bird
did hover above Osiris
to take him within
did such a love convulse upon the Nile
as I-mm-eti and Ab-Mer the outlaw
throughout the nighttime found Hathor
's wild flood
drowning the tramples of the spear men
searching the marshes for Ab-Mer
cursed the Pharaoh.

But morning found the laughter of Hathor twisted to groan
and doomed with separation, danger, dread of death
Ab-mer slipped down the Nile, through the Delta, and off
to an island, crying every day for years and years
but losing the grasp of the love lost tragic

And I-mm-eti made a mistake
one night drunk on henek, the barley beer,
and the child grew within
and she was seized enslaved by a mean man
who smelled of burnt goose feathers
for a life of never a dance.

Ab-Mer was able to return from exile 20 years later
during the senility of King Annenemes I
but could not find his love

though he searched from cottage to tent to hut to house
both sides of the river
but no one knew her, remembered or thought to find.

And as for the Risen House of Hathor,
when Ab-Mer returned it was many years
since the great fire wiped that down into the
sand   and the great art lay beneath the claws of
the griffin vultures.

And Ab-Mer secured a postion
in another House of Life, more sedate
more powerful, wealthy, modest
where Ab-Mer became a staid bent disciple
of rectitude. "I lost my chops"
he'd moan beneath a load of
wine, railing against the Nile-side water stick
foreboding drought.

The aged drunken Ab-Mer
lowered his weeping face to the table.

Then
"Hathor!" he cried, "Hathor
I shall dance!" and
the old man
rose to dance, and dancing
tore some sinews
in his legs and
stumbled to the floor where
purple bruises spread
beneath his dry barked skin.

"I-mm-eti" whispered Ab-Mer
"O I-mm-eti."

HIEROGLYPHS

Each word a
flash-pod correspondent
to an event
in the Great Beyond
or the Yaru Fields
as in the
possibility of Coming Forth by Day

the hiero-symbol

Keep that grain
swooning
Hathor, please!

THANATOIDAL
TRANSFORMATION
EQUATIONS

"Thou com'st out of thy grave every morning
Thou return'st every evening
Thou passest through eternity in pleasure"

by the living swarmies
painted on papyrus

by the hiero-symbols
painted 'pon basalt

to   the Beyond

soul scroll

in a box
wrapped
in the mummy cloth
or stuck into the coffin

        believing that
        the words
        and pictures

        would ensure transreal
        grooviness for the snuffee

No greater belief in
words has there been.

I WANT TO BE PURIFIED

I want

to be purified

in the

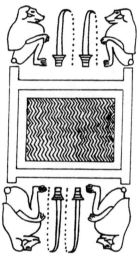

she sang

THE SINGER

The blind harp strummer
sat before the vizier's banquet
singing of shrieks and shrieks
and thoughts of shrieks and symbol shrieks
and new shrieks bouncing surly
down upon the faded shrieks of faded pain

"Hang garlands on the neck of your wife
and garlands on her arms,

and listen overhead" sang the blind Egyptian harper
"and listen underfoot
and sing when there is silence
and sing when there is safety
and sing sing sing"

        While 4600 years later
        there once was a singer
        and a writer of songs
        who worked in a bar far off
        near Blabtos, Georgia

The week was up and the singer walked
into the office of the club
collecting he hoped the rest of his
pay
        which had to be given him
        all in cash
        according to the terms of his contract
        with the club

The owner looked askance
at the tired grimy person of tunes, he
snorted down from his nose just as
he hooted smoke from his mouth
and the gray boiled downward, disappeared

                The sheriff's been
                looking at the wheels
                of your van and they
                don't look none too safe

                Besides you sing
                ugly, little man
                your band belongs
                in a high-school basement

                We reckon a hundred dollars
                and a free trip out of town
                ought to do you right good.

But you owe me 300 dollars!
Sweat was breaking out upon his long
black sideburns

& his eyes were wide with piss-off
sweat too spread over his blue satin shirt
wherever there was hair beneath

And the band's got to get their pay
Mr. Parsons!

No mind to me
son, he replied
I don' give no frig
for those tub thumps
call themselves a band

But those hundreds of folk
who came! What about
them? Hunh! My customers
come for to guzzle
boy, don' forget it
guzzle! guzzle!
Now take this hundred
and get   and don't
go howling to my cousin
over at the union
neither.

Sheriff! He's in here
givin' me some lip.
And watch your badmouthing me
hear?

I ain't going out of here
till you 'fill the terms
of my contract. He pulled
the wadded wet-with-sweat document
out of his back pocket
unfolded it & held it
up to the light—I'll have to sue

Give me that! the owner snarled
and grabbed it out of his hand
tore it shreds

The singer
knocked the owner down
locked him
shirt pulled up his back
saw the white kidney—
twinge of evil, singer couldn't

stop his hand   hack the
fatty mountain—aiee! the
head of the owner flipped back and forth
lips slobber pain.
Help! Murder . . . kidneys! Sheriff!

The sheriff banged open the
door, door edge thudded
the singer's side
He pulled them apart   then clubbed
the singer with the gun butt
thomp! thomp! Goddamn greasy
little pretender. Why don't you
get a haircut? I heard you, off-color songs
mixed up w/ church songs. You got
no right to put on an act like that.
Mr. Parson's right to pay you what
you deserve

   Now get on out of here
   in that van of illegality
   you call a home—

And the sheriff
pushed him
staggering for balance out of
the club, past the sweepers bent
in the sawdust, into the
alley.

With sounds of ptuh! ptuh!
he sputtered the blood from his lips
and started the engine
then let the steel-guitar player drive
when he got the urge to sing
and crawled into the back of the van
where he pulled a guitar off the wall
and sang with throbbing mouth of cuts
almost till dawn
when the van pulled up at
a motel near the Tennessee border

BOOTY

Like a dog-breathed homunculus
the wizened child crawled along
the cedar sluice

        squeaky rumbled the dyspeptic colon
        and no wonder so
        for they froze the growth
        kept the boy like a monkey
        fed vulture scraps

        "Gotta keep li'l Mek-mok small"
        quoth dad.

The cedar plank tongue
slowly had slid   150 feet   through Princess Her-Wetet's
mountain tunnel
not touching any sides or floor   lest the trigger
tumble the mountain liths

His father, older brother, grandpa
waited at the sunlight
for the child to load the booty upon the sluice sledge

Fruition! Fruition! the grandpa rubbed his hands in glee

        "We will
        pull out the plank
        the little brat
        will try to run
        out toward us, then . . ."

For 75 years the robber clan of Mek-Macrae
had tried to crawl
through Her-Wetet's smooth straight tunnel
into the Theban mountain

but the designer had fiendishly
set traps at regular spots
on the walls and ceiling and floor
that a light passing foot or pressure on the wall would
trigger an avalanche of adios,
tons of the mountain

Mek-mok the boy had lost his uncle
and uncle's uncle two different times
they tried—dead in crush liths.

The Tomb of Princess Her-Wetet,
Chantress of Amon:

Cedar sluice-tongue
'pon which the boy
crawled into
The Hall of Booty

Surface

Tunnel
Entrance

BOOTY

Seals
of
Royal
Snuff-works

Three remaining
triggering devices
on floor. Above each
is a hollowed cavity
containing tons of rock.
Rock inserted by
sealed shafts
leading to surface.

Triggered
booby containing
skeletal remains
of Mek-mok's
uncle (cleared
before insertion
of sluice-tongue)

The finest   Lebanese planks
built end to end
like a medical spatula
for some huge deity such as Ptah

with sides built
up with edging
(prevent the sledge
full of looting
        fall off the tongue
        trigger any rock plop).

The boy crept through the murk with
tallow torches
            toward the moolah

along the well-oiled sluice
dragging the small sledge
150 feet of rope off either end.

        Mek-mok slowly loaded the satchels
        from the treasure room of Her-Wetet's tomb
        upon the sledge
        and the robbers at the entrance pulled
        it to the light
        then Mek-mok reeled the empty back for reload.

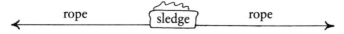

The boy was (slightly) daffy
smashed a miniature granary
with a ceremonial oar

            disturbed vibes
            upsetting the Princess
            by means of those
            THANATOIDAL TRANSFORMATION EQUATIONS

as she was plucking 'ternal wheat
down on Paradise Farm

The Nubian reapers
bent in Yaru pleasure alongside the Princess
　　　just as the boy was chopping up the tomb

fell down groaning
their mer cutters splaying
　　　princess bent in agony

Robbers didn't care, they
sought the jewels, the gold
and yes　the precious oils

Mek-mok was sloppy
oil jugs rolled off the sluice
smashed

　　　one in particular indicating
　　　that the Princess was burned
　　　by the Regal Perveyor of scents —
　　　not oil, but ooze unholy
　　　village struck by flash-plague
　　　such stench

phew!
　　eyes smarting, nose like snorting
ground-up Brillo pad.

Mek-mok ice-picked the rubies from
the statues of the Princess

　　　A scream of pain
　　　in the grain fields of Heaven
　　　"My eyes!　my eyes!"　red pits
　　　where eyes had.

　　　Transformation　transformation.

"Canst 'ou see now
in the Yaru River bottoms

Princess dear? Hyuf hyuf hyuf" im-
portuned the griseous-fingered thief boy

pried the gold leaf off
the coffin sledge, broke the alabaster jars
dry friable guts of Her-Wetet
spilling on the row of sacred oars.

The rob boy stuck   a couple of gold wheat stalks
into his mouth thinking of fangs
laughed, "Look at me! Look at me!"

Will Her-Wetet walk a pauper through Elysium?
Forever adrift
          in a reed boat
reft of the total pleasure
promised by the words of the walls
down upon the howling banks of
the *RIVER*

REPORT

DATA! ᗡ ᗡ DATA!

Subject: Her-Wetet
           Chantress of Amon

Case File: Dimension $X_{147}^{\circ} - 44739J$

Time: 1153 B.C.

Place: Necropolis, Thebes, Egypt

Subject was a female Hamitic, 5'11", Bl/Br, approx. 140 lbs., age 37—cause of death: stampede of hippopotami. This writer attended various nodules of the embalming ceremonies. Subject was afforded a full 70-day spice douse, wherein subject's features were held remarkably intact.

A report of the yaru Surveillance Team is attached below as *Appendix A:*

Imposition of the Netherworld Glyph   ⊕   occurred in 70 days. During this period the coffins and artifacts were carved and painted. The texts of the Book of the Dead, 'dorned with the fair *beauté* of Her-Wetet torrid chantress, were drawn up in 7 colors 'pon the wide papyrus scroll.

70 days to ⊕

Brain was hooked out through nose
    some of it dissolved via dissolve-gush poured within
      brain thrown away, no care fo' rotting data files

    heavy chop scene
      performed on bod
guts disgorged   mummified   placed

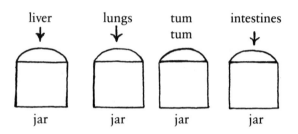

liver   lungs   tum   intestines
                    tum

jar   jar   jar   jar

    in graven alabaster
    protected by the 4 sons of Horus

    these Canopic containers put
    upon a sacred slege

post scrape job re inner much gush
cavity packed with pieces of natron salt
(sodium carbonate sodium bicarbonate
sodium chloride   sodium sulphate)
wrapped in linen
      suck up body ooze
        body drool
natron sprinkled on the outer also
—dry Egyptian climate helped the dry-out

After the jerkification, natron removed
body given water sponge bath
then rub-a-dubbed with resins coniferous
cavities packed with resin-soaked wads o' linen
—stuffed with taxidermist's care: "Life! Life!"

Stan Brakhage, Eye-Form Surveillance data positor

filmed the sew-up
stone eye
    placed on chop scar
    prior to the long winding

fingers, toes
wrapped separately
toe stalls   finger stalls
of gold
    coatings of resins
    applied to coatings of linen
    175 yards of linen strips used
    to wrap the subject chantress
    Her-Wetet.

        There was a slight
        but savable error
        —portion of the right ear
        was discovered beneath
        the chop bench
        swept up, according to the
        ceremony, with the spilt
        desiccative and linen pieces extra,
        buried in storage jars
        near the mouth of her tunnel.

    By barge procession
    passed
    right bank to left bank, Nile
    down into the Valley of Salient Snuff

oxen pulled
the sledge

        mourners fisted dirt in poofs,
        self-beat, shrieks
        & long dinny moans

friends of Her-Wetet, plus

priests and servants
and porters with platters
of gifts.

By the edge of the tunnel
last ceremony
coffin
tipped on its end

"opening of the mouth"
that the chantress
yodel gently
down where the scoffers
cannot scoff

Priest in role as Deity
drove out the
devil dirt, like
    "out thou 𓏤𓏏𓈎𓃂 fiends
    out thou hitler verbs
    out moloch out nixon out
    of this voice!"

APPENDIX A.

Report: Yaru Surveillance Team
Subject: Princess Her-Wetet, Chantress of Amon

Eye-Form Surveillance Team
was required to utilize
Beckmanian
Transformation Nodes (via diagonal dimension dives)

in order   to hover behind
the Death Barque   while
still escaping the particularly wary wet-fanged
        attendent Deity known as Anubis

The jackaline Anubis
is thought to be able to undertake a nearly *n*-
dimensional scientia sweep
so it was necessary to observe only from
those dimensions he was unable to fathom.

Her-Wetet, the Chantress of Amon, was observed
in the rapids of showery rubicund petals just prior
to being sucked into the golden eyeball wherein the
petal torrent falls and disappears. It is stunningly
beautiful to see the soul brain fall through the Eye.

Dimensional Adjustment Procedures enabled the
Eye-Form Surveillance Team to observe the Princess
arriving in the first sections of the Underworld.

When the rope of the Ferry was thrown ashore
a cat-headed goddess (holding a whip) led the singer
toward and through the so-called Door of Percipience.

Hallelujah
        the deceased   strolled quietly past
        42 fierce Spiritual Assessors

        Soul-jewel shining
                no sin-grime cloying
                                Hallelujah

        Osiris reached in between her breasts
        and brought out her heart

        Jackal-headed Anubis
        lifted her heart
                upon the scales
                heart on one tray
                against the Maat feather
                on the other

                Little baboon jumping
                up and down on the midpole

while Ibis-headed Thoth wrote down
the data on a tablet

Concomitant with the weighing
was the chanted enumeration of sins *not*
committed

(if th'accumulated sin-grime didn't tilt the
heart against the Feather then

Heaven!

but if it tilted, then soul—and it is confusing
here—would either a) be doomed to roam Earth

b) be consigned to the fiends of
Adios Chew Devour
the so-called
⸢𓂡⸣-fiends

c) be eaten by a low-slung
wrinkle-snouted Devourer
known as Am-Mut

d) all of the above.)

Blameless in truthful blessèd bliss-out surged
the sinless Chantress of Amon when her heart
balanced the Maat

Osiris tucked it back within
her bounteous bosom

And the low-slung
wrinkle-snouted slime gobbler Am-mut
had to wait for ano'r time ano'r soul
to suck from the plate of truth.

Subject chantress then endured the marvel of the Final Purification
in the Lake of Fire
guarded by 4 apes holding torches—

4 torches extinguished
in the 4 pails

of Universal Milk . . .

It is to be noted here
that *all* this judgement was hard indeed to
bring to surveillance:

Shifting Forms . . .
unable to
jot them
as they shift . . .

Dream-Stream
film just blurrs:

What is she doing?   The subject chantress and baboon
                      of Thoth adore the Solar Disk

No! No! Dummy!   The subject chantress is actually
                      bowing down before the supine
                      deity: Crocodile Earth

Bull Shit!   The subject chantress is being led
                      by the triune Ptah-Osiris-Sokaris
                      for induction into the Mysteries

Hear the chant of the priests: "That she may
make all the transformations she desires"

Forms   Forms   Form   Forms

Apparently jubilant over her new abilities
subject assumed a razzle-dazzle arpeggio
of weird forms:
            microbe, heron, swallow, ox
            mollusk, rainstorm, church
            steeple, projective verse

            what a dazzling sequence!

And more: subject Her-Wetet on Ra-raft
             subject Her-Wetet as Sky Bug

then Ra-Hawk   Solar Disk
Sun Flower   Cherry Blossom

She might have volunteered for a tour
of duty as an oarsperson
on the Solar Barque
            but one of the strangenesses
            of this particular paradise
            is that they settle down, the souls,
            to reap bright grain in a
            brass-walled place
            called the Yaru Fields

            where the Spirits are precisely 10′6″ tall
            where the grains are precisely 10′6″ tall
            and the grain-ears precisely   3 feet long

            said fields
            located in the 2nd Arit (or Mansion)
            of the 7 Arits
                        Underworld.

Accordingly, Her-Wetet settled down to a normal death
and walked toward Yaru.

There are twin sycamores
of malachite at the world's end
twixt which

        Ra oozes forth

There is the Western Mountain
where Hathor Cow
goddess of necropolis

            met the snuffee
            saying "Hi!
            the grain field's that way!"

        Image shift: celestial bull and 7 kine

4 rudders of He'v'n
Shu muscling Nut off Geb

"Hi, Hathor!" — the soul of Her-Wetet
beaconed in thrillsome shifting tides
of form and form

Then Her-Wetet happ'ed to walk past
godly Osiris lying on his back
on the loamy mount of Khepri

The festal cone of Her-Wetet melts
in the fire of their pleasure
Her-Wetet atop the God
belly burning.

Subject chantress was not hesitant in fact frequently
to interrupt her wheat-cutting activities in the eons
thereafter and to run over to Khepri Mountain
and to effect unification with the deity known as
Osiris (a Male Black, about 19'6", weight approx. 430 lbs.,
with extremely bloodshot, maybe entirely rubicund, eyes,
wearing blue beard and blue wig, armed with flagellum)

Scarcely had subject
begun to work in the
sun wheat when subject
bent over   as if in pain
her eyes   looked like
the insides   of ketchup bottle caps

Subject winced —
The wheat field
where she and her
companions (unknown
Male Blacks wearing Nubian
wigs and armed with scythes)
were deep in harvest,
fell apart   in disarray.

Dimensional Scan Operation
indicated a forcible intrusion
into her mountain tomb-tunnel
by the robber clan known as
the Mek-Macraes
where certain stones were pried
from votive statues, a
model granary was beaten
t'toothpicks therein.

Subject cantatrice rolled moaning down.
Her body bent
a long row of grain
with
        falling rolling
that the sun wheat heavy
struck muffled gong sound
against the Yaru Walls of brass.

Subject stumbled forth
along the River Bank

"My Eyes! My Eyes!"

20,000 A.D.

The Council of Eye Forms,
a liberal, nay even radical, body of
intergalactic deities

composed itself upon various mutually agreeable
dimensions—namely those dimensions denigrated
by some, not in the Council of course, as "useless
Thrill dimensions" but nonetheless, a suitable
series of dimensions for communication among the
members of the Council of Eye Forms,

the purpose of the meeting being a general tactical
discussion of the aeon-long "Apopis problem"—
now that Apopis had apparently been caused to crumble
into desuetude in the so-called

> "14th-emanation dungeon
> of gutted phantoms."

In the texts

Apopis was always stun-stomped
but like
an angry maniac
or stare-at-me! psychopath
        strode-slithered
        forth   forever & a day
        to the boos and hisses
        of th'blobs
        of conscious molecules.

1) execration

2) sympathetic magic
        were the traditional scams

by which the priests
paralyzed Snake

at the "critical moment"

when Snake

was going to

chew the lightnings and erg sprays
off the sun
like a flower

to leave
a vermiform sky-ice
scene   for

the apparent purpose of
the self of him
to writhe in worship
of himself as the Total.

With a corona of fabricated TV broadcasts
a long eel in coils
of knife-stabbed red waves
upon the nadir of encroachment,

what a struggle, in lives & gore & misery
it was
   to tap those blades
      into the rolling back
         of Apopis.

Accordingly, and be it remembered that this is just
a tale, the Council
held Snake 'neath the fierce administration of
      an n-dimensional
         milky way μώλυ
            or trance moly.

Silence reigned where shrieks were once the revenue.

Drops could be heard
in the golden chalice

       it was so silent
       upon the belly of the
       All.

    But
    the august sere angst-heads
    ᴐ ᴐ ᴐ ᴐ
    ᴐ ᴐ ᴐ
    ᴐ ᴐ ᴐ
    debated
    far too far into the "night"

    the question of Apopis

e'en with the knowledge of so many trillions of ex-cons
(Council term for the expansion-contraction of the Big)
when Worm rode berserk—

but now! lay stunned
within his current form of
    175,000 miles of star-shine snake grease.

    Think upon it earthling:
    to rid the star pelt all
    of gore gobble.

    For a' that and a' that
    the good Council
    shed tears

       o'er the death-hacked Apopis

    though Apopis
       spat hate
         & crests of destruction—

"Each morn
he tried to bushwhack
the sun

arising in
the arms
of perfect love!" railed

the prosecutor
Eye Form.

But eve time
found the Hate Worm—
knives in his back jangle-jiggling

ready to
suck the yummy fires

of

And pray to know why the Council of Eye Forms
did hesitate to snuff forever
vengeful, violent, remorseless

street punk
on the avenues
of the Universal Hole?

"Dost 'ou *really* really pine for Apep*
be a lawless field fluid of crazed gravity?"

sang a languid Form   nicknamed the Coma in
many a set of dimensions.

And many shuddered indeed at such a "thought."

* Another name for Apopis.

Meanwhile the trance moly waned.
and pity raised up the child of pity,
manumission.

Turgid, then slowly warping
then faster faster faster

Apopis rolled, coil 'pon coil,
out of the dungeon
shrieked and cackled
farting clouds of revenge,

spitting a promise of Merry Pain-mass
to all the beastie bands of molecules

grew out of the nature of mad Sky
to stare and dare and be aware
beloved 'pon beloved.

WHY HESITATE TO KNOW
ALL GENTLE THINGS

THE THIRTY-FOURTH YEAR

Today read *Steelwork*, by Sorrentino,
100 Selected Poems, by E.E.C.,
The Metaphysical poets,
    esp. Thomas Carew's
    "An Elegie upon the Death of the Deane of Pauls,
    Dr. John Donne"

Made a list of letters to write,

        1)   2)

            3)

      4) 5) 6)

Worked on 6 short stories.

To know that
mirth supplies divisions

To live as tense art
watch friends lie in a bathtub of blood

D.A. Levy call his mother
    say he's going to go to S.F. work in the P.O.
    or maybe kill himself

    on the monuments

Dave Hazelton with whom canoed out to
confront Polaris submarines 1961
1968 came back from Amsterdam
    saw him one day he lost his teeth
    jumped from the bridge gone the
    editor of Synapse Berkeley 1965.

So it's there
like an alphabetical file
of autopsy reports
can't face life like a fist fight
must crawl down lonely arroyos

Rain washes the rodents down the sluice
Fire wipes the Bronx

And to watch Richard Nixon
trying to summon pity as he goes
into the hospital, same room as Johnson
heart attack—probably wired w/ special
lines—a bedside red telephone
so that if he should suffer swiftly
maybe die, he could still phone in those
S.A.C.'s & Minuteman missiles
squelch the world.

a) to float along
b) to become a dandy
c) to practice as a scholar
d) give up, get farm
e) to prepare a list of books to
   write this decade, proceed
f) push self toward ego dissolution, peace-in-practice,
   serve, lick stamps forever in a mailing
   room of protest bulletin
g) bowery
h) make movies only, or maybe write a 40-year opera-poem
i) give up literature, write a manifesto about a
   new mode of painting, sneer, work hard on canvas,
   decorate spaceships
j) found a radical socialist quarterly—muckrake,
   poetics, sedition
k) Phil Whalen: copy everything he does

B'day
August 17, 1973

HOMAGE TO LOVE-ZAP
for Judith & Julian

I know that the robot
is struggling to form itself
            to chew into death
           the leaves of the rose.

I know with my soul-eye, the spirit of the fascist sewer
tries with its might

           to teach all mammals
           to live as garbage—

   so that the muscleless lumps
        lie down in the metal cans
        & beg for the lids to be lowered.

    I know that it is useless
    yet with my last breath
    I shriek   I raise my fist
    I shout showers of love-bursts above the
                 golf carts
    I violate the dictates of the werewolf freaks of war
    I circle up with lover friends
    to drive to distraction the uncreative circuits
    of the robot fist.
    Every day is May Day when you dance the dance.

  Things line up to block
  the molecules of my imagination
  but I just add them to the frantic clutter!

Come O love-zap
Come O thrilling never-seen
           imaginations
Come and take me 'pon thy thrilling rides!
Come and take me
Come on come on come on.

PAUL

In 58 & 59
fresh out of Mo.
as a nascent beatling
cowering in the Café Figaro
    after Greek class

reading *Beatitude*
and the early *Evergreen Review*

one of my goals
was to meet Paul Blackburn
& to become his friend.

    It was a definite pleasure
    to purchase his
    early books

      The Nets,

  & Brooklyn-Manhattan Transit

        down in the
        superversepower basement of the 8th
        St. Bookshop.

And later there were the readings.

        He had such dedication
        to the spoken
        poem

           Who can forget the
           readings at the 10th St.
           Coffee House, at Les
           Deux Mégots, or at th'
           Le Métro Café

say 1964
ahh that such
peace of verse
should flow again
down 2nd Avenue
the cobbles.

If you listened at all
in 1963
I bet you can still
hear his lines &
breaths & cadences

I loved to hear him read

you could *feel*
his line

The way he could chant
with that deep base line
almost like a held vowel
underneath

the words . . .

The way
he could
click open
his Zippo lighter

as a punctuation
right in the middle
of a poem
to light up a Picayune
puffs pouring out of his mouth
as further punctuation.

He faced
the terror
it seems to me
with such tender grace.

I sometimes hear the
flashes of his conversation
filled with poesy's sun folk—

say, how much awe he felt for the work
of Robert Kelly, and worried for his health

and the anecdotes, he told them with glee,
about the time, one night, Tim Reynolds . . .

I remember he wrote a poem
celebrating someone who'd first turned him on
to Bols gin
           a few empty brown ceramic bottles of which
           sat on his window sill
                      attesting to the thrill

& he'd recommend it
           your way
           as gin-flash

           & he'd make sure
           you knew where to
get some special coffee
           beans he knew about
           for that morning
           pre-verse   wire-up

                     1964
                     gave me
                     directions how
                     to locate
                     some of those
                     long thin
                     notebooks
                     in which he
                     was writing
                     his Bakery Poems

an extraordinary obscure
little stationery store
up in the 20s
off Lexington Avenue.

I can close my
eyes & see him again
19 E. 7th   his
2nd-floor apartment
with those remarkable
shiny sanded floors

& in the back, his work room
off the kitchen

a long neat shelf of tapes
above the desk

He must have taped
two hundred readings

(& yes the memories of sitting
down at a table just about to read,
to look nearby, hey! there's Paul
bent down near the floor, winding
fresh tape upon the reel!   )

And he *knew* his tape recordings:

he'd tell
you about
some introduction
you once made to a poem
in a reading you'd long forgotten

& both you'd chuckle
afresh
again.

& when you left his house
　　he always said, "Peace."

　　The problem is
　　that it's just too easy
　　to say something like
　　"the sad molecules convulse in the mist"

　　or that the supernova
　　supersedes —

　　But they can't take
　　his voice away from us —
　　yes — I'll have hot cider
　　w/a cinnamon stick — in
　　my mind again —
　　I can hear his voice
　　any time I want

　　It is late spring
　　1964

　　The tables are crowded
　　with nervous
　　poets clutching
　　their spring binders

　　the coffee
　　costs too much

　　but the words are free

　Paul is reading
it is a good night

　　　and like a
　　　good percussionist

　　the poet clicks open
　　　the lighter
　　　in the cadence.

THE AGE

This is the Age of Investigation, and every citizen must
   investigate! For the pallid tracks of guilt and death,
   slight as they are, suffuse upon the retentive
   electromagnetic data-retrieval systems of our era.
   And let th'Investigators not back away one micro-unit
   from their investigations—for the fascist hirelings
   of gore await in the darkness to shoot away the
   product of the ballot box

And if full millions do not investigate, we will see the
   Age of Gore, and the criminals of the right will rise up
   drooling with shellfish toxin, to send their berserker
   blitz of mod manchurian malefactors mumbling with
   motorized beowulfian trance-instructions, to chop
   up candidates in the name of some person-with-a-serotonin-
   imbalance's moan of national security

And this is the Age of Investigative Poetry, when verse-froth
   again will assume its prior role as a vehicle for the
   description of history—and this will be a golden era
   for the public performance of poetry: when the Diogenes
   Liberation Squardron of Strolling Troubadours and Muckrakers
   will roam through the citadels of America to sing
   opposition to the military hit men whose vision of the
   U.S.A. is a permanent War Caste & a coast-to-coast cancer
   farm & a withered, metal-backed hostile America forever

And this is the age of left-wing epics with happy endings! of
   left-wing tales/movies/poems/songs/tractata/manifestoes/
   epigrams/calligrammes/graffiti/neonics and Georges
   Braque frottage-collage-assemblage Data Clusters which
   dangle from their cliffs the purest lyricals e'er
   to hang down a hummingbird's singingbird throat

This is the age of Garbâge. And we're not talking here about
   Garbâge Self-Garbâge—but an era of robotic querulousness—
   how at the onset of a time when the power of a country

is up for grabs, the Garbage Hurlers, attired in robes
of military-industrial silk, arise to hurl, as swift
in their machinations as a chorus in the Ice Capades:

and none of us will trudge this era without a smirch-face
      waft of thrilly offal dumped upon our brows of social
      zeal—and the pus-suck provocateurs armed with orbiting
      plates of dog vomit will leap at us while we stand
      chanting our clue-ridden dactyls of KNOW THE NEW FACTS
      EARLY! Know-the-new-facts-early, know-the-new-facts-
      early! And do not back away one micro-unit just because
      some C.I.A. weirdomorph whose control agents never ended
      WW II invades your life with a mouthful of curdled
      exudate from the head of the Confederate Intelligence
      Agency &

This is the Age of Nuclear Disarmament—when the roamers of
      the Hills join hands with the nesters of the Valley
      Wild, to put an end to nuke puke w/ a zero-waver total
      transworld Peace Walk—that the War Caste wave no
      more their wands of plutonium and the dirks
      in the nuclear mists no longer chop
                                    up the code of life

And this is the Age of the Triumph of Beatnik Messages of Social
      Foment Coded into the Clatter of the Mass Media over
      20 Years Ago!   Ha! Ha! Ha! How do we fall down to salute
      with peals of Heh heh hehhh! That the Beats created change
      without a drop of blood!

      In 1965 it was all we could do to force-cajole the writers
      for *Time* Magazine not to reinforce the spurious Anslinger
      synapse, that pot puff leads to the poppy fields—
      but now the states are setting hemp free! Ten years of
      coded foment! Heh! Heh! Heh!

            Yesterday: the freeing of verse

            Today: pot

            Tomorrow: free food in the supermarket

Heh! heh! heh!

And finally let us ne'r forget that this is the Age of Ha Ha Hee!
Ha Ha Hee is such a valuable tool
in the tides of social transformation!

Ha Ha Hee will set you free from worm-farm angst
Ha Ha Hee will even curdle the fires of jealousy!

Ha Ha Hee outvotes the Warrior Caste
Ha Ha Hee doth whelm the self-devouring quarrel

Ha Ha Hee peals out through all the cosmos
    mandorla'd with

            poet angels holding Plato's
            7 single syllables
            in a tighter harmony than the
            early Beach boys—

This is the poets' era
and we shall all walk
crinkle-toed upon the smooth
cold thrill of Botticelli's shell.

Written for
the New Year's
Reading at
St. Mark's Church
January 1, 1975

Three Sections From
INVESTIGATIVE POETRY

I

We will see the day of

RELENTLESS
PURSUIT OF DATA!

Interrogate the Abyss!

To go after an item of time,

(as Olson says; p. 134 of
The Human Universe & Other Essays,

the essence is to
"KNOW THE NEW FACTS EARLY.")

(After all, wasn't one of the shrieks of our generation
to suck eternity from the NOW, to hear in Sonny Rollins'
saxophone, to hear in Snyder and Burroughs, to hear in
meditation and mountain caves, the beauty of the present,
of instant gratification, of word wheel and world wheel.)

Therefore, how in tune with our era it is
to open up a case file on an item of current time,

and, to quote Olson again, this time
to say that history is "Whatever happens,
and if it is significant enough to be recorded,
the amount of time of the event can be
minute."

minute!!!!

To surround an item of time
with thick vector-clusters of
Gnosis,

to weave a corona
of perception through verse
and through those *high
energy verse grids* which
we mentioned earlier.

II
Investigation Glyphs.

Draw a graph or glyph
of your investigation target

surround the glyph
with gnosis-vectors

pointing to the target

and never surrender!

robot targeting

    knocked away

        get on feet

            prepare new question lists

        approach the target
        again again again

        The Item of Time
        forever caught & exposed
        & explicated

        in the thews & thongs &
        melodies of bard-babble.

ahhh sweet nets
of bard-babble.

III

Concerning Shyness
and Investigative Poetry.

                        data
                     data cluster
        data cluster   data cluster   data cluster
data cluster   DATA CLUSTER   data cluster
data cluster   **The Big D**   data cluster
data cluster   DATA CLUSTER   data cluster
        data cluster   data cluster   data cluster
                     data cluster
                        data

To *unpeel* the data clusters (to get to the Big D)
as well as to fashion into skeins of syllables
and vowel melodies and poesy.

People with shyness problems
who want to
get into investigations
have a great obstacle
to overcome.

Do not be afraid
to one-on-one
your Data Target
in the abyss.

And do not hesitate
to open up a case file
on anything or anybody!

When in doubt,
interrogate, rhapsodize a weave,
or Q-quilt or question list.

"If a man or woman does not live
in the thought that he or she
is a history, he or she
is not capable of
himself or herself"

saith Olson,
p. 28 of *The
Special View of History.*

AND THE GENERALS

And the Generals
with wolf masks

crowded about
the bomb

to seize it from those
who had made it

& Hathor
was angry

WHY HESITATE TO KNOW

Why hesitate
to know all gentle things?
And then, this:
to feel again your "skin fins"
as you have determined it.

To make Law
of our amours,
free again.

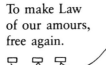

To read again

of thee and thine.

Across the
purloined space

To crochet
our desires
into the silver stomach
of the numinal
tundra.

Yazzah!

Yes: once again,

yes,   yes,   yes.

LOVE & THE FALLING IRON

I

Keats is dead, and Fanny Brawne
who, in his letters we can see,
crawled away from his embrace (& he from hers),
hackly & T.B.-coughed; how sad
when the tubercular hawk scratched
out the bristling hard-on's flesh
& the drooling verbs
                of meat-mate
walked away like walking verbs
                ﻬ   ﻬ

                of ancient glyphs.

How sad to fall in love so much
that you don't know the date of
the train you're on. Or whose
wallet it is you pay the champagned
waiter.   But I'll not smirk w/ trivialities.
The lines of the panties' elastic on thy thigh
O Rebecca Wright, is something I have
never seen save in thy poetry. Yet
too many times have I famished lain
and thought important angels made
my mind boil sad aloof; and oh I sang a rueful tune
upon a harp; or was't a dirge of desolation
struck on the frets of a wheelchair wheel?

Is this too sad? or cloyed of gibberish?
I don't know, but the levels
of reality themselves are cloyed with
legs & breasts & arms & eyes
which jut, like fragments in an aspic,
down through the layers, some in some,
others in others, and reality is bound
by these layered pegs
to one sad sandwich (which we love to eat

and spit our layered juices mouth to mouth).

The biggest gift is bravery, to
lift up the hand to bid the
genius. And this: to know what to
do, to beg or to borrow, or
to die like Herman Melville,
clerk at the docks.

Remember all your loves in a row,
my love? What a motley crew
they are, each face in the glare
of a tensor light. But ahh let's
switch off the lamps, my love, and
let us examine again our
loves in the not-so-gloomy
light of our organs' files.

II

Forgive me God if that I ever
wrote a book called *Fuck
God in the Ass*, which I did
indeed. And just last year, she
pictured me on my death bed
trying to argue with God o'er
some dumb book of my youth
which Jesus found assaultive
to the Grail.

But I think of this, O God,
a movie I heard someone
made in the '60s (I never saw it):
a shot of the orphans
of Vietnam perhaps,
splashed with a demon barrel
of jellied gasoline, burning,
sizzling, demoted to tissue.

And then: the sound track (sing it with me, please)
"Jesus loves the little children
all the children of the world"

& you will understand
the title of my book, which
first I heard from the mouth
of Theodore Berrigan, who'd heard it himself
from the mouth of a poker player
I believe in Oklahoma—or maybe in
the Navy; he used it quite a bit
in the course of a game, or a hand of.

Yes,
to end a sentence on a preposition
Charles O.: to beg a chapel
once again in which
to pray thy safety's sake
on the airline of the

falling iron.

       & is not everything a preposition?

& the Chapel of Prayer
& the Castle Perilous
& the Visionary City   a cluster of phantom genitives
                       after the OF, perhaps,
                       down near paradise, for sure,
                       but not too far, my friends, from
                       the wonderful music of muck.

                       "The wonderful music of muck?" thou
                       snickerest.

                       Or dost 'ou hate muck?
                       or dost 'ou hate thy God
                       for hitler's soap?
                       or dost 'ou hate the
                       opening bass of Mingus-ah-um?
                       or dost 'ou hate the
                       C.I.A. with all thy heart?

or dost 'ou hate the
guides who say there is no
Visionary Spire; who drool
the apothegms of Sartre
into thy children's television eyes?
or dost 'ou hate the
food chain & dost 'ou hate
each fox that bites the rabbit babe?
ahh muck, ahh muck
the wonderful music of muck.

SAPPHO'S POEM BEGINNING
Φαίνεταί μοι

Equal to the gods
is the man who sits
in front of you leaning closely
and hears you sweetly speaking
and the lust-licking laughter
of your mouth, oh it makes my
heart beat in flutters!

When I look at you
Brochea, not a part of my
voice comes out,
but my tongue breaks,
and right away
a delicate fire runs just beneath
my skin,

I see a dizzy nothing,
my ears ring with noise,
the sweat runs down
upon me, and a trembling
that I can not stop
seizes me limb and loin,
oh I am greener than grass, and
death seems so near. . . .

THE CUTTING PROW
For Henri Matisse

He couldn't paint, he couldn't sculpt. He was confined to a
wheelchair and gripped with *timor mortis*. From his bed at night
he'd draw on the ceiling with a long stick with crayon attached. Yet
somehow he adjusted his creativity, finding a new mix of the muses,
so that from the spring of 1952 through the spring of 1953, in his
final creative months, he was able to produce some of the finest art
of the century, a group of wall-sized works of painted paper cutouts
—works such as *The Swimming Pool, Large Decoration with Masks,
The Negress, Memory of Oceania, Women and Monkeys*, and the
smaller *Blue Nude* series. He thought he could scissor the essence of
a thing, its "sign," as he termed it, as if he had vision in Plato's
world of Forms.

The genius was 81
Fearful of blindness
Caught in a wheelchair
Staring at death

But the Angel of Mercy
gave him a year
to scissor some shapes
to soothe the scythe

and shriek!   shriek!

became

swawk!   swawk!

the peace of
scissors.

There was something besides
the inexpressible

thrill

of cutting a beautiful shape—

for
Each thing had a "sign"
Each thing had a "symbol"
Each thing had a cutting form

—swawk swawk—

to scissor seize.

"One must study an object a long time,"
the genius said,
"to know what its sign is."

The scissors were his scepter
The cutting
was as the prow of a barque
to sail him away.

There's a photograph
        which shows him
sitting in his wheelchair
bare foot touching the floor
drawing with crisscross steel
a shape in the gouache

His helper sits near him
till he hands her the form
to pin to the wall

He points with a stick
how he wants it adjusted
This way and that,
        minutitudinous

The last blue iris blooms at
the top of its stalk

        scissors/sceptor
        cutting/prow

(sung)

Ah, keep those scissors flashing in the
World of Forms, Henri Matisse

The cutting of the scissors
was the prow of a boat
        to take him away
The last blue iris
        blooms at the top
                on a warm spring day

Ah, keep those scissors flashing in the
World of Forms, Henri Matisse

Sitting in a wheelchair
bare feet touching the floor
Angel of Mercy
        pushed him over
                next to Plato's door

Scissor scepter cutting prow
Scissor scepter cutting prow
Scissor scepter cutting prow
Scissor scepter cutting prow

        ahh
swawk swawk

        ahh
        swawk swawk

        ahh
        swawk swawk

HYMN TO O

There was a term
　　of Anaximander's
inflamed my youth
　　τὸ ἄπειρον
The Uncrossable
The Boundless

& really, for years, went batty
　　for τὸ ἄπειρον

used to think
all the time about the Apeiron

Peace Eye, my book of verse, was part of it
Eye-Heart-Minds
　　　　shooting the rapids
　　　　to vanish in the Lake
　　　　outbound to Peace Eye
that was part. To make
poems history again—that
was the sum.

Anaximander graphed the thrill of the first map, the
"perimetros," as they called it.

I had a vision
after Olson's death
of two different things

One that he walked up
to a twisted circle of rope
with the ends lashed together
where they met—

The shen-sign of Egypt
sigil Aeternitatis

and leaped through it
as if it were a tire swing

the second, that somewhere somehow
when that famous ferry's pole struck
the brass shores

      he ran into a posse of
      pre-Socratics

      who drew him
      that is to say, forthwith!

      into a delicate discourse

   There can never
   be enough of dignity
   when bards
   fly flash
   to the
   shore.

I can feel you Charles
when I stare at the froth
of Gloucester's tanny rocks

You're there, next to the O-Boat,
talking with Alfred Whitehead

Anaximander is there
holding a
10-dimensional sphere

A lone Ionian column
stands on a hill
I see you O
bending at the base
writing a line upon the whiteness

You dive, again again
like a dolphin on ancient silver
through the shen-sign's ring.

Anaximander
with a perimetros
of "Earth & the Sea
    & the Sphere of the Sky"
and the Endless Oatmeal
fo the Apeiron

Hey Charlie O Charlie
Olson has entered
the cartouche

and this is a prayer
that he and Anaximander
walk down through the fields together

O what a map they will make

RAMAMIR

A Tune for the Pulse Lyre

It was the fall of
'58 when
we met in Greek class
at N.Y.U.

She was there
because of an interest
in archaeology

& I that my mother had
said that a gentleman
reads Greek and Latin

(plus, who could scan
Pound's *Cantos* without them?)

She was 17; she'd been
the valedictorian
of her class
at the Yeshiva; and
when we waited by
the elevator after class
she had the habit
of twirling one whole turn
in her long red
Chesterfield coat
with a belt
and two big white buttons
in the back.

One afternoon
as we walked across
Washington Square
past the large gray circle
of the fountain

I said, "I guess
we'll have to join the Beat Generation."

"What's that?" she asked.

It was just about then
I gave her the nickname
Ramamir

We used to hang out
in dusty bookstores
and in coffee shops
to hear the poets read

She wore those stylish
spear-toed high heels
or Alan Block
high-lace sandals

She wore black kohl
around her eyes
and a leather vest
laced up the sides

Her black wool turtleneck
held heaven's heaviness
She was my blond-haired
diamond sutra

And when we made love
by the Central Park zoo
ahh the gods above
they watched us loving

And the policeman
standing on the bridge too
He watched us loving
by the Central Park zoo

It was so intense
we soon forgot
the detectives her father
hired to follow
us around
because I wasn't Jewish

I wrote poems about her
and shyly showed them
over Café Viennese
at the Figaro

with lines like
"She was the night
and the moon through her eyes

was as white
        as the drapes of a
    marble statue"

            or

"Ramamir grabbed the long moon
in her teeth and dashed home
to devour in her den"

    & other lunalalic
            phantasms
    beaming from Ramamir's eyes

For seasons
her home was hell
as her parents
tried to stomp us down

And sometimes it seemed
as if demons
were driving bonkers stanchions
to cage us apart

Ahh Ramamir Ramamir
my kohl-eyed rebel girl
somehow we persevered

and now we make maple syrup
on Mead's Mountain Road,
sap spiles dripping in praise
of the force
that brought us together.

MY BOAT WAS OVERTURNED

My boat was overturned
It was hard
to set it right

when part of me
loved the waterfall
and part the land

At 5 A.M.
I sat on the bed
with my face bent forward
into my hands

wondering how
to get out the door

to you

THE ART OF THE ELEGANT FOOTNOTE

The art of the elegant
footnote is ever to
be practiced

    (a pig farm mentioned
    in the Maximus Poems is
    no longer there—so the
    elegant footnote describes
    the pig farm from the minds
    of those who remember)

A footnote is a dangling data-cluster
muck like a shaped piece of metal in
a Calder mobile

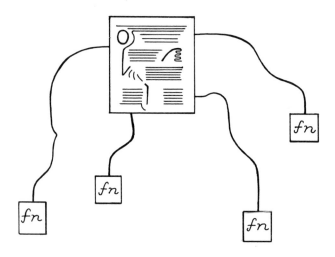

YOU WERE THE ONE I LOVED

You were the one I loved
watching the solar barge
on tenth street

We stood to gaze at the heavens
to watch for the sun boat's oar
over tenth street

oh it's wrong to speak   of freedom   and peace
unless   your love   is justly done

I could weep I could moan forever
for the wrongs that I have done
on tenth street

but there's no turning back the time-stream
to be a better man

You picked the wildflowers darling
and pressed them in a poetry book
                (for your dirty bard)

Tenth street is burnt and gone
but you and I still love as one
and the Eye of Peace stares on

CEMETERY HILL

Twenty-four years have gone
and I see you still
standing in your black suit & veil
on Cemetery Hill

They say   some day   in the solar wind
giant ships shall sail
There'll be no thinking then   how lovers fail
their fortunes to bind

In the sky above   the foggy lake   the boat set sail
bearing my mother away
to the end of the sky   where they stub out the torch
                  & they empty the boat
on the shores of the Lake of Fire

            They stub out their torches
            in pitchers of milk
            on the shores of the Lake of Fire

            They stub out their torches
            in pitchers of milk
            on the shores of the Lake of Fire

There've been so many many   broken hearts
the sky should be red
but the solar wind   oh it didn't care   & we didn't dare
our fortunes to wed

but twenty-four years have gone
and I see you still
standing in your black suit & veil
on Cemetery Hill

1981

WOUNDED WATER

and what's the Work?
To ease the pain of living,
Everything else, drunken
dumbshow
  —Allen Ginsberg, "*Memory Gardens*"

I have swum for twenty years
in the creeks of Wounded Water
and the tears that I have shed
are swallowed up in Wounded Water

All the faces   of those who've gone to harm
reflect around our faces
staring 'bove the roil
                of Wounded Water

Swaying in the water, amidst the lily leaves
tangles of telephone wires
and smashed guts of tape recorders
waving and weaving and swaying
in the glut of Wounded Water

O the files! once so full of data-gnarls
lie chaotic as a marble's marls
and folders of sleaze   blow in the breeze
and the pages drop   to float then plop
beneath the brink   of Wounded Water

The oceans of grief slosh by slosh by
the pylons of anger and harm—
We may hope to defy and disarm it
or snatch another from the fire,
just before we drown
in the gully of Wounded Water

Ease th' pain! Ease th' pain!
and stand, with art, that elegant plier
in the torrent, rising higher,
of moiling, roiling Wounded Water

In di Gasn, Tsu di Masn

(INTO THE STREETS, TO THE MASSES)

SAPPHO ON EAST SEVENTH

Poet John Barrett is a graduate student in the classics department at New York University. His obsession is Sappho. There are drawings of her likeness on the wall, as well as photostats of fragments of her poems found in papier-mâché coffins in Oxyrhynchus, Egypt. Barrett's translations of her poems are given prominent display above his desk, and the living room has been converted into a workshop for the construction of an ancient four-string lyre with a sounding box fashioned from the carapace of a European tortoise. He's managed to acquire about a dozen shells. They're all over the pad—tortoise shells on milk-crate bookshelves used by his friends as ashtrays. He eats his morning oatmeal out of a shell. The time is late summer 1963. The place East Seventh Street near Avenue A.

> He had an obsession for Sappho
> He lived inside her meters
> like a trout in running mirth
>
> He was building a four-string lyre
> to sing Sappho down
> Sappho come down
>
> He copied lyres
> from the Parthenon frieze
> looking for the perfect shape

> There were tortoise shells
>   hanging by nails
>   on the wall
> Another lay on his desk
> near scraping tools, a saw,
>   a pot of glue,

some whittling knives
from H.L. Wild.
Goat horns
were hard to get
on the Lower East Side

so he carved the arms
from the legs
of an armchair.
found in the street

and a thin rounded sounding board
cut he   (from a spruce-wood shingle)
to fit
on the shell

The crossbar from arm to arm
had tuning pegs from
an antique broken banjo
found in the trash
of a burned-out store

A bridge he
shaped & notched
from an ebony comb

and when he had built one
with which he could sing
he scribed it with Sappho's
Ἄγε δια χέλυννα μοι
Φωνάεσσά τε γίγνεο
"Come my sacred lyre
make yourself sing"

The Lyre
   transformed him—
      in the mode of the

Dada masks
   transforming the shy young poets
      in the Zurich cabaret.*

Barrett became Some Other Bard
      striding through his rooms
      holding his lyre
   singing with all the passion to summon:

"There is a river
in Mitylene
   where Sappho
      used to swim
         with a friend

dropping their sandals
with ivory inlay
      at the water's bank

I saw Sappho
bending in the foam
peplos-less and chiton free
      on a summer's day

      singing a song
         that is lost

*Referring to the Cabaret Voltaire of 1916 and the spontaneous
poem and dance performances inspired by the donning of Marcel
Janco's famous masks.

They later lay
in the
creekside glade

soothing each other's
skin
    with oil & caresses

singing a song
    that is lost

    O Sappho come down
    Sappho come down."

A friend from school,
    Consuela,
        lived next door

and heard John Barrett's prayer
        through the tenement wall

She listened each night
    to dig what it was
        and finally understood

    when Barrett Sang:

"as a glider
    swoops down
        from the cliffs

over the birchen hills

        swoop thou down O
Sapph' swoop down"

She lay in bed
    with her ear
        to the wall

spiss-hissing with held-back laughs.

She mocked him:

"as a cornflake
        through the
            subway grate

into the
        bubble-gum
            muck

            settle thou down
            Sapph' settle down"

The next day   she told her Greek class
Together they plotted a trick

One night she would
appear on the fire escape
she shared with Barrett
—attired in chiton and peplos*
and sing/chant some Sappho

as if she were Sappho's *geist*

She bought a bolt of white linen
on Orchard Street
and brocade for the edges
of Ukrainian symbology
            at Surma on 7th
            & sewed herself Sapphic attire

She memorized the Hymn to Aphrodite,
Consuela,
            to sing Sappho down
            Sappho come down

*The basic attire of ancient Greece, both garments being fashioned
from oblong pieces of cloth. The chiton was a tunic of linen or
wool worn next to the skin, doubling around the body. It was
pinned over each shoulder and held at the waist by belt or cincture.
The peplos was a heavier cloaklike overgarment.

It was late afternoon when she
came from the shower, donned the chiton
and peplos overgarment,
crawled upon the windowsill, shoved
aside her boxes of flowers

—she knew it was the hour that
                    Barrett would sing—

and crouched upon the gritty
black ironwork
                    blistered and pitted
                    from 20 coats in 90 years.

When she heard Barrett's loud
prayer begin and the strings
of his lyre resound, she

stood to sing—Consuela
saw the air above the fire escape
come apart—as if some giant hand
had scissored a line
in reality's tarp

There was a chirping of birds
and dim dots clouding the view.
Through the pointillist gray
an arm was thrust,
                    holding a lyre,
then another arm—
                    the fist of it clenched

then opened, and tiny kernels
fell upon the grate
of the fire escape
to rain on the courtyard below

Conseula sank in awe,
the rungs of the fire escape
streaking her knees with grit-gray stripes

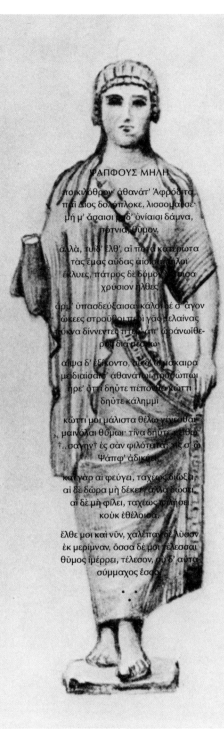

ΨΑΠΦΟΥΣ ΜΗΛΗ

ποικιλόθρον' ἀθανάτ' Ἀφρόδιτα,
παῖ Δίος δολόπλοκε, λίσσομαί σε·
μή μ' ἄσαισι μηδ' ὀνίαισι δάμνα,
πότνια, θῦμον,

ἀλλὰ τυίδ' ἔλθ', αἴ ποτα κἀτέρωτα
τὰς ἔμας αὔδας ἀίοισα πήλοι
ἔκλυες, πάτρος δὲ δόμον λίποισα
χρύσιον ἦλθες

ἄρμ' ὑπασδεύξαισα· κάλοι δέ σ' ἆγον
ὤκεες στροῦθοι περὶ γᾶς μελαίνας
πύκνα δίννεντες πτέρ' ἀπ' ὠράνωἴθε-
ρος διὰ μέσσω·

αἶψα δ' ἐξίκοντο, σὺ δ' ὦ μάκαιρα
μειδιαίσαισ' ἀθανάτωι προσώπωι
ἤρε' ὄττι δηὖτε πέπονθα κὤττι
δηὖτε κάλημμι

κὤττι μοι μάλιστα θέλω γένεσθαι
μαινόλαι θύμωι· τίνα δηὖτε πείθω
†..σάγην† ἐς σὰν φιλότατα· τίς σ' ὦ
Ψάπφ' ἀδικήει;

καὶ γὰρ αἰ φεύγει, ταχέως διώξει,
αἰ δὲ δῶρα μὴ δέκετ', ἀλλὰ δώσει,
αἰ δὲ μὴ φίλει, ταχέως φιλήσει
κοὐκ ἐθέλοισα.

ἔλθε μοι καὶ νῦν, χαλέπαν δὲ λῦσον
ἐκ μερίμναν, ὄσσα δέ μοι τέλεσσαι
θῦμος ἰμέρρει, τέλεσον, σὺ δ' αὔτα
σύμμαχος ἔσσο.

* * *

while Sappho's body
seemed to float
        through the tarp-warp gap

the very second Barrett's
edge-of-frenzy voice
sang

        "Sappho come down
        come down Sapph'!"

At first John Barrett
        tried to
gaze at the apparition
with an it's-about-time expression

        Then, "Sappho!" he gasped,
        for actually
        Barrett had little trust
                in the summoning power

of a lyre with arms
        from a scroungèd chair
        and a tremulous voice
                more like a dare

        He glanced about his di-
        sheveled beatnik apartment
        and wished he had cleaned away
        the bottles from the night before

Sappho picked up his lyre
        from the desk
                setting her own aside
                and started to sing

He could *see*
        the words she sang
above her
        with a throbbing life of their own

Words of Water

άθάνατ'

Words of Fire

Words of Broken Oars

When the song was over
        Barrett stood stunned
                tears on his cheek

sinuses cloggy, vision blurred,
ache of love in his stomach.

Then she walked to the wall
        where he'd pinned
                his translations

He tried not to glance
        at her breasts
just as he did not look
                in Stanley's Bar
                        on a midriff summer night

The bosom
        of a ghost
                is not for the kisses
                        of eyes.

Barrett was horrified
      to see Sappho stand
            reading her verses' versions

It was hard to keep from
         ripping them down.
Finally, she turned away, & laughed,
          "Better than Byron's—
             at least."

Next she visited his shelves
        "Let me gaze upon your
        Book Boat," she said

Oh, no!
     thought John Barrett,
worrying about the many marginal tomes
           in his Book Boat

The gibberish of friends,
       the smut, the
           malmarked scholarship.

     Sang then Sapph':

"There is a boat
      for every bard
bobbing in the waves
      a Boat of Books

Some will say
      to build a boat of death

Others will sing
      a trimaran of green

But a bard
      had better build
           a Boat of Books

      for the troublesome
        flow.

And you shall find
      a Muse for your age
           in the Book Boat prow:

        Retentia
    Muse of the Retained Image.

The panpipes
      the seven-string lyre
           the arsis & thesis—
     The muses
      with which I sang

     but yours is the era
        of captured sunlight
           & oxide-dappled tape

Rententia
catches the beauteous flow
swifter than a cricket's foot

The photos taped to your wall
of my poems' shreds
                were wrought by
        Retentia

She rushes to the aid of groaning Clio
whose scrolls lie thickened & black

She helps you to sort
                to soothe
                        to winnow

        as well as to keep
                to save
                        to shape.

The Image is safe
        with Retentia
                for a million years
        till the pulsing fires
        which scorch all lyres

                O
Once on an
incurved hillock
        near Mitylene
a circle of maidens sang
        — Alcaeus was there

        if only
        if only
I could hear
        their image again!"

Sappho stopped singing
        There was a near-sob tremble
                in her voice

"Pray to Retentia, John Barrett,
for each muse aids
                    in her measure
and the task
            is to know
the mix of the muses' gifts
                    in your lines."

She moved her hand to the wall
            to touch the photostated papyrus
            The wall cleaved apart
                    and forth stepped Retentia
            in a blue-black gown
      crackling on its surface with
            tiny jiggle-jaggles of lightning
      which seemed to form
            almost a lightning lace
                  above the blue-black weave

Barrett was wondering
            what sort of prayer
                  was proper to utter

            in praise of a new muse
                  standing in his room
                        from the Book Boat prow

He was foolishly thinking
            of scooping the floor
                  to kiss Retentia's hem

when Sappho walked to the kitchen cupboard
                  and opened the doors

"What does she want?" Barrett asked himself.
            "I don't have any Methu," he said,
            inwardly praising himself for his wit.

(Methu was a famous
            wine produced
                  in ancient Lesbos)

"Have you no herb-scented oils?"
                 she spoke in complaint,
            shutting the cupboard doors—

      "How frailly you fail
      in matters of love
      & longing," she said

      "How can you think
      a woman like Louise
                 would love you,
      knowing what you know?"

She entered Barrett's bedroom,
            a tawdry chamber
                 with its mattress
                      on the floor
                      'mid candle spatters

      and a blue print of Sappho's
            face, large as the wall,
                 above the bed

"Now you shall learn
            the Rubbing of Oils
                  & Glossa Didacta."

      Retentia
appeared at the door
   bearing a tray of
      tiny Canopic jars

   —oils & unguents
      with which Sapph'
         could ply her hands

      as she slid the
clothing from shy John Barrett's
skinny frame
      & rubbed him thrillsomely
from jar upon jar
         each oil having
      a different thrill
         —a mild sting here
            and a tremble there—

      & sweet smells
         mixing with
         smells piquant

   "There is much you do not
   know,"
         spoke she,
   neatly hanging her peplos
   upon a nail on the door
   after she had shut it

   She drew Barrett down
   O Barrett come down

   "We have called it
            the Glossa Didacta
   and every bard must have
            its perfect knowledge"

Down sank they
upon J. Barrett's mattress

She pulled his poorly combed
badly washed curls
down upon the only thing substantial

It was like a softened rosehip
The rest of her was ghost-mist

"Your head is the rudder
& I shall steer it over
the rapids,"

this way
that way
steering with fondly grabbed ears
steering the rose bud
steering the bard boy's brow

showing him pressures
motions
patterns

"That's it
That's the way
That's perfect"

clitoris bifurcated
like
a
lithops
(left side to the right brain
right side to the left brain?

twain
bundle
of come-nerves?)

Lithops bella

She came in words arcane,
Sapph'-sighs writhing above her
in jumbles of
      hieroglyphic neon,
    as when she had sung—

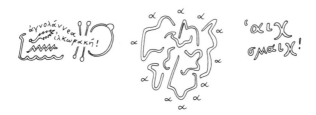

She spoke to him in Latin,
"Now I have taught you
      the Lingus Didacticus
and those you coax
      into its trembly thrall
shall know a dance more lightly tapped
than the meters of Euripides."

Then she bade him
    come inside her.

"Don't you make it only with, uh, *gunaikes*?"
    he replied, breaking into Greek.

She'd arranged Chianti bottles
                around the bed
                        with flickering candles within

Barrett looked up
        to see the shadow
                of the ghost
against her blue print image
                on the wall
as she tugged him gently
                but insistently
till they lay
                face to face
        & she guided him up & within—

an hour
        to make him
                believe anew in the
                        thought of the Numen

or an hour
        as a catalpa blossom
                floating in the River Thrill.

                Ahh, *côte à côte*
                he longed to lie
                with her
                upon the dawn—

        "Stand up," she said instead,
        "We're going on a journey."

        "If so," replied John Barrett,
        "give me satyr legs!
        yes, sturdy hairy legs
                & hircine hooves
                to spring and leap!"

Sappho smiled, but
could not comply.

She held his hand
& floated
from the room on East 7th

above the green copse of
                Tompkins Park

dizzily dizzily
whirling a further era back—

to 1911
where Emma Hardy sat alone
on a spring morn
                at Max Gate*
her husband downstairs
correcting
        proofs
                with his mistress.

They entered Emma's bedroom
through the dormer windows
There was a feeding station
                by the sill
                        for the birds

Sappho felt pity
                for bitter Emma Hardy
                        whose husband's hands

were ever poised
        to trace the
                curves of youth.

She was trying
        to ready herself
                for the day

*Max Gate: Thomas & Emma Hardy's house in East Dorset,
Dorchester. In 1908 Emma had ordered dormer windows built in her
attic boudoir, outside of which the birds at the feeding table would
flock to eat from her hands.

but her face
    was twisted in pain
      from a torturing back

The pain was too consuming
    for her to lift
      a plate of crusts
        to the birds

She rang for her helper, Dolly Gale,
to brush her hair
Dolly stood behind her
    unbraiding untangling uncoiling
    the sleep-jammed tresses

The slightest tug
    of the bristles
      brought agony's gasp

till Sappho reached out
    to place a soothing palm
      on Emma's spine

    to ease away
    the axing ache

"The oil, John, the oil," Sapph' urged
and John Barrett parted the robe
    from the painèd shoulders

and began to caress
    with Mytilene's finest
    from a thin-necked jar.

The peace in her back
    brought the first smile
      in months

"Call the birds for us, please Emma?"
Sappho asked, and Emma Hardy
    walked to the sill
      and raised her hands

Emma was 68
Emma in pain
Emma threw open the dormer
to feed them her wedding train

There must have been a hundred birds
in a wild gustation of feathery blurs
above the feeding station
            pecking the breakfast crumbs

"This house Hardy built," Sappho said to
John, with a tone of disgust,

        "without a hot-
            water tub!"

She took his hand again—"Prepare for a trip
to A.D. 642"

There was a further whirling
after which
            they alighted
at a site of steam & fire

Barrett thought for a moment
they might have followed
Dante and Vergil
            into a bolge of hell

There was a hairless man
with a shiny skull
& a missing tooth in front

throwing bundles of papyrus
scrolls
            into the word-eating mouth
            of an open-hearthed ceramic furnace

Water boils above it
            in a large copper basin,
feeding through ducts to a

                    series of copper tanks
of varying stages of heat
so that a bather in
the pool can tug a string
for the heat of her choice.

     Stacks of scrolls
               jut this way and that.
     Barrett cranes his head
               to read the names
                    upon the next thatch
                         to be tossed

     Oh, no! It takes a few seconds
               reading the run-on script
                    for John to recognize
                         the plays of Aeschylus!

     They are heating the baths of
     Alexandria
     with the last of the ancient
     libraries

"Look!" she cried, "do you know what that is?"
The attendant had an armload of volumes*
with projecting knobs. "He's just about to burn
the final set of my collected works."

The fireman
tossed them two by two in the fameless flame

Barrett tried to grab them
but his hands brushed through
like mist into a redwood bough

               "Some of my poems were
               torched by Caesar

*Volume: from *volumen*, papyrus rolled around a stick or sticks, the
text written in narrow columns.

burning the ships in
Alexandria's bay
    & the fire reached ashore

Some were chopped into
papier-mâché for the
middle-class coffins of Thebes

Some were destroyed
when surly Christians
sacked the Serapeum*
in 391

And now it is time
for ashes and chars
to come to the
    mixolydian mode

Some poets' words
are written on water
Others make flame
    to make it moil."

Just then
    the voices of women
        & the clack of clogs
           were heard

The daughters of General Amrou†
    had come to soak
        in the steam-topped pool

& to smooth
    with pumice bars and strigils‡

---

*One of the two ancient archives in Alexandria.
†Amrou seized Alexandria for the caliph Omar in 642. The latter, it is said, ordered the remaining books in the ancient library destroyed on the grounds that now that the Koran had been written, they were no longer needed.
‡Curved scrapers for removing bath-softened skin.

their steam-soft skin

The women
    passed their towels
       to their servants

and the high-domed room
    was soon resounding
       with laughter and aqueous splash

All of a sudden Sapph' shoved past
       the sweaty man by the furnace
and gathered the final rolls,
    to Barrett's gasp,
    and flicked them into the rage

She turned, disrobed
handed her chiton to
       Barrett

and slid into the water
to sit on a marble plank
      with the damozels
      in the moil pool's midst

"Hotter, hotter," she urged
the attendant, tugging on the rope
to empty a torrid tank
      upon them

      while out of the furnace
      a burning fragment fluttered

just a corner of paper,

curling & burning

with Sappho's last word

βρεθεῖω
flaming
βρεθεῖω

It fell at Barrett's feet
He tried to stamp
            at the fire

            to no avail

A silver knob
    from the end of a scroll stick,
worked in a pattern of porpoises,
            rolled out of the furnace
    all that remained
    of the works
    of Sappho of Mitylene

Barrett reached down to seize it
            He slipped
                & smashed to the floor.

He came awake
        in his pad on East 7th
and saw a foot on
        the fire escape.

"Sappho!" he half-screamed
            and rushed to the window

but it was Consuela
        in her Orchard St. chiton and peplos

She seemed asleep
        but opened her eyes at once
            when he touched her

She told him her tale
He told her his

showed her
the silver knob

and the smell of the top of his wrist
                    still thrillsome
with Sappho's oil.

    Afraid, yet
        unable not, to
            talk about
        it

    Barrett told portions
    to some, &
    the whole event
to a few

    with the silver knob
    as carefully shown
    as a saint's bone.

    To some
        he was
            Crazy John

("You sure this wasn't
        the head from your
            grandfather's cane?"
                Sam Thomas sneered)

    To others
        he was
            Lucky Bard

(to carve the proper lyre
        to sing Sappho down
            Sappho come down)

Though he sang her each eve
he saw her no more
till later that year
on a snowy night

John saw Sappho
her neck laden
with heavy
Russian crosses

praying in the deep drift snow
on Avenue A

before it was disturbed
by salt & sweep

outside the redbrick
St. Nicholas
          Carpatho Russian
church

Icons were
melting in
her hands

& rubies
dropped
from her
crusted neck
into the snow

(though later
          they vanished)

He ran to see her
She was weeping

          "You'll cry too"
          was all that she said

& she walked
away into the blizzard

weeping & wailing

& Barrett
never saw her again.

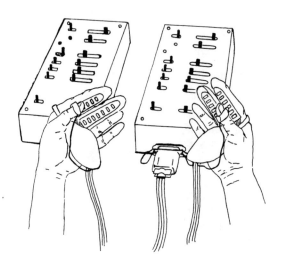

drawing of Pulse Lyre by Miriam Sanders

THE FIVE FEET

You can always fight the foulest grief
with drinks and thrills
You can channelize your septum
with thousand-dollar bills

But you better get obsessed again
on the Change Wheel's rungs
or they'll let the tumors grow
in the hummingbird's lungs

You've got to have five feet
to skitter down the road

One foot in the grave
One foot in the glitter
One foot in the gutter
One foot in the glory
One foot near the Grail

Lawrence said to build a Boat of Death
upon that main
Well, you'd better patch the leaky Boat of Life
call it Paradise Plain

There's nothing wrong with writing lines of verse
on a foam-flecked oar
Even if we cannot join Matisse
through Plato's door

You've got to have five feet
to skitter down the road

One foot in the grave
One foot in the glitter
One foot in the gutter
One foot in the glory
One foot near the Grail

HYMN TO MAPLE SYRUP

The leaves from
the wet black sugar maples
hang down in the icy fog—
just a few—
the color of blanched-out butterscotch,

above the weed-spiked snow.

& the pine tree's bough
springs up from the snowbank
where it was jammed for months
and nods up and down,
spraying the air about
with a fine shaking
of icy granules.

The sheet of ice across the creek
is cracked here and there.
The creek depth has dropped
since midwinter rains
and an eery foot-high gap is left
'tween ice and icy flow.
You can see it in the breach
where the deer drink
and the blue jays hop for a dangerous sip

Soon giant tiles of it
will begin to drop
from the ice floor
down upon the blue stone roil

and it's time to boil.

My pockets are cold with short metal tubes called
spiles

with a knob-like protuberance
on upper edge
to keep the sap bags
from falling off.

I feel affection for the
rough swirls of ancient maple bark

for each giant sugar
            is a Patting Tree

and sometimes I stop
to hug a maple as huge
as two people reaching
around it,
sliding my arms past
spile scars of seasons past,
dark circles
        in dark crusts
the winter mittens touch,

and then to lean
with brace & bit
the knob of it
            pressing the chest,
and chew through
the gray to the butter-tan wood.

The wood-curls at the hole's mouth
turn moist
as soon as I screw
out the drill bit

Then gently to tap
the spile in the hole
& the sap runs shiny
out of the shiny tip

while sliding the sap bag
upside-down

then twisting it
straight so it's hooked
on the spile.

Some trees are big enough
for more than one
and sometimes I worry that plastic bags
will tinge the sap with pollution

Across the creek
is an open-front sapping shed
with an old Norge stove
once gas, but now
outfitted for wood

I've draped it over winter
with a plastic sheet
to ward away rust.

Time now to rake the leaves away
& set up the stovepipe flue
(stored in the garage)
which curves from the stove and up
then angles at 90 degrees through the wall
then up again to a
tin-hatted hood by the roof

Inside the Norge
are two lines of concrete
laid front to back
and topped with a

row of grills
that look like hibachi grates

I lift them away
and shovel the ashes
of last year's final fire
from the trough beneath

Most of the shed is saved
for a gnarly stack
of branches and boards
much of it windfall
& some from the Woodstock dump

the game is to make the
syrup for free.

Today I raid
the neighbor's woods for
fallen birch

skwonching through snow
to drag a tall white log
in a hesitant lurch
across the blue stone property wall
pennants of loosened bark
flip-flapping white on white

& the long end leaving
a deep dug furrow
like a giant possum's trail

down to the Norge's mouth
to be chain-sawed.

The correct beatnik hour
for emptying the sap bags
is 2 A.M.

Back & forth th' galoshes skwonch

scaring the deer
from the yew-berry bush

I rotate the bag on its spile
and pour the sap in a metal pail
then walk through the dark
to the 40-gallon holding can
by the shed

steady steady
dodging the low hanging white pine's
bough as the raspberry wands
and the China rose whack the legs

trying to keep the sap from sloshing
with little frothy waves
to douse the knuckles and gloves

as cold as the ocean at Gloucester.

It's a fine aerobic sapper's trudge
a fourth of a mile or more
tree to can to tree to can
till all of the
bags hang
flaccid again.

There's a long rectangular pan
with handles on the ends
for the stove top
from the Kingston China & Bar Supply

I pour a few gallons
to fill it.

It takes so long to
build a fire!
as if the gnarl-pile's kindling
were haunted
by a water haint.

I want it now!
Flames! Forthwithity!

I love to boil at night,
beneath the sap shed's single bulb
from the ceiling,
keeping the Norge's door wide open
and stuffed with overlength wood.
The first rush is sweetest and best
they say
and so it is tonight
as the room width fills
with billows of paradise steam.

Tending the boil I sit
out there on
an old oak school desk-chair

working on poems or tales
to bulb light and Norge light
like jotting notes
by the forge of Hephaestus

pausing to flick the
shiny skuz
that roils to the top of the pan
to a corner
with a slotted spoon

learning to love the sp-u-lappp of it
sp-u-lapping the barren floor.

Or you can put on a fresh tray
then go to the house
            to type a few poems
but you have to be careful
to return in a hurry
to add more logs
and flick the skuz

Tarry too long
        over *Star Trek*
and you'll lose the sap
in a caramel ooze

It's sad to have to hurl
a hissing tray of sap gravy
down into the creek, kneeling
to scrape long scabs of carbonated
black
from its sides.

It takes about
an hour
to boil away a pan

You learn how to tell
how close it is
dipping a spoon for a taste

or you know how low
it must be
to be nearly done.

The mittens & potholders
reach for the handles
and turn

the tray to the side for a better grip,
quickly,
for the flame tips rise
through slits in the stove top
singeing the hair on the wrist
'tween glove & sleeve,

the steam so fierce
it sears the eyes
so I close them, turning slowly
determined not to slosh syrup
onto the floor, or worse,
and walk four steps in blindness to
a table in back
where I tilt the tray so the sap pours out
of a corner
            down to a metal pot.

For a second I open my eyes to
sight for the pour

and then the "spoawwt!"-sound
of sudden syrup
            on chilly steel.

I set the tray-pan back on the fire
then rush to dip fresh sap from
the can

before the tray doth burn.

I boil up another batch
then pour it too in the pot
till it brims

and I carry it over the bridge
to the house
bring back another pot
and on and on
till I quit at the dawn.

You have to be careful
stunned at sunup
walking with the final boil
toward the creek
eye brims red
      from facing the steam
not to trip on the mulberry stump

or slide in the slosh
of the railless bridge
with blobs of 210-Fahrenheit syrup
sizzling your tissue.

Back in the house
it's the peace of ZZZZZ's,
the smell of maple
        in mustache & hair
& reddened wrists from the sap sun.

The next evening Miriam & I
finish it off in the kitchen
half-gallon by half-gallon
heating it up to a boil
then checking the temperature.

(First you see where water boils.
It varies according to pressure.
Most days it's 209.5 or 210, but
some it's 211 or 12. And then
we add another seven degrees,
for our height above the sea,
and that's the maple-syrup point)

We use a dial thermometer

clipped to the pan edge.
Sometimes the eyes get again
a hint of the pain of a
lobster's eyes
leaning too close to read
the sugar-crusted dial.

Then one of us holds

a hammock-shaped padding
        of cheesecloth
hand to hand
while the other pours the
syrup through it
into the jars to be sealed.

Some years the
sap keeps coming & coming & coming!

a never-ceasing flood
        to be boiled
and I feel guilty
if I let any spoil
till finally I yell,
        "No! No more!"
and pull the bags from the trees
and pry off the spiles
with a hammer's claw
& twig up the empty holes.

And then it's done
for a year.

        Coda

There's nothing to it.
It's like the ocean
or a raked Zen sand.
It's empty. Yet full
of the best.

It helps you to set
aside the fear
of lumps in the skin,

to leave all that was
and toss all that will
in the sweet roil of foam
in a tray on the hill.

YIDDISH-SPEAKING SOCIALISTS
OF THE LOWER EAST SIDE

They came when the Czar banned the Yiddish
           theater in 1882
They came when the iron-tipped Cossack's whip
           flicked in the face of their mother
They came when their parents were cheated out of
           their farms in Vilna
They came to escape the peasants at Easter, hacking
           with scythes and knives
They came when the Revolution of 1905 was crushed
They came when the soldiers broke up their socialist
           presses in Cracow
They fled from Siberia, dungeons and work camps,
           for printing leaflets and fliers—

        pamphlets and poems and leaflets and fliers
        to spread in the workshops
        spread in the streets
        spread in the factories

        in the spirit the era had spawned
        the spirit the era had spawned

           "*In di gasn*
              tsu di masn
           Into the streets
              to the masses"

They came to Antwerp and then to London
           and then to Ludlow Street

        to make a New World
        inside the New World
        at century's turn—
        The Yiddish-speaking socialists
        of the Lower East Side

Some remembered
        with pangs and tears
                the beautiful rural life
                        wrested away

Mushroom hunting in the dampened woods
Bundles of grain in the carts
Market day in the shtetl

Some strained their eyes
for the gold-paved streets of the West
just to be greeted by one of those
"incomprehensible economic collapses"
that New York gives to its poor

The East Side
        had been slums
                since the overcrowding
                        after the War of 1812—

but the tenement rents of 1903
        were higher than
                nearby "better" places

Two thirds of them owned by speculators
getting 15 to 30 percent (or more)

so that a family of ten
        was jammed
                in a two-room flat
plus boarders!

till a leafleteer
        in desperation
                laid aside his ink

to open a curbside store
        with a gutter plank
                and 3 brown bales of rag

Or they carried the cribs
        to the hallway
              to set up a sweatshop—
They were not alone

From thousands of windows
        came the clackety-clacks
              of foot-treadled sewing machines

and the drum-like sound
        of long-bladed scissors
              chewing on oaken boards

and the lungs turned gray
        with tidbits of tweed
and the red-hot irons
on the tops of the coal stoves
to smoothe out the bundles of cloth

and the sweet gulps of air
        on Cherry Street
walking out kinks of the legs at dusk
from a day at the torturing treadle.

A rose curved obliquely on the stalk of the hammer.
The Lower East Side
was the strongest socialist zone
        in the United States
for the first twenty years
of this century.

It was a
        wild world of words

and everywhere
        the song
              of the wild lecture

arose above a wild lectern—
Scott Nearing

        at the Rand School of Social Science
Morris Hillquit
        at the Workmen's Circle
Emma Goldman
        at the Educational Alliance
Eugene Debs
        coming in from Terra Haute
                to Webster Hall

And political discussions
        on the summertime roofs
                in Yiddish, Russian, Polish, & English—

        wild world of words

Labor Day parades from East Broadway
to Union Square
Cousins on the floor
        from fleeing Siberia
                after the Revolution of 1905

Union meetings at the Labor Lyceum on E. 4th—

        Flashes of the Ideal
            in murk
                in muck
                    in mire

Talking all night at the Café Royale
            at 12th and 2nd Avenue

        after the Yiddish plays at
        the Kessler or Tomashevski Theaters

Garment-worker rallies at Cooper Union

Joining the Women's Trade Union League
Fighting for a shorter work week
6½ days to six, and then
to 44 hours, on the way to 40

        Flashes of the Ideal

in murk
in muck
in mire

In di gasn
tsu di masn

To make a New World
inside the New World
at century's turn
the Yiddish-speaking socialists
of the Lower East Side.

For twenty years the East Side socialists grew.
They filled the arenas
and packed the streets

though those who stand
in the bowl of shrieks
know how the bowl
stands silent
so often

when the votes are
counted.

There was a party in the streets
The Lower East Side had never seen
the night in 1914 that Meyer London,
whose father had worked in an anarchist print shop,
was elected to Congress

They danced and sang
through Rutgers Square past the Daily Forward
till the sun blushed the color of communes
above the docks.

Meyer London served for three terms
until the Democrats and Republicans in

the State Assembly
gerrymandered his district.

In 1917 the Socialist Party of N.Y.C.
sent ten assemblymen to Albany
and seven to the N.Y.C. board of aldermen
and even elected a municipal judge

while Morris Hillquit
pulled 22 percent of the vote for mayor—

It looked like the Socialist surge
might move as a spill of thrills
out through the state

> *In di gasn*
> *tsu di masn*

to make a New World
inside the New World
        at century's turn
the Yiddish-speaking socialists
            of the Lower East Side

And then, in the spring of 1917
            the U.S. Congress
                voted for war

The socialists
        met in St. Louis
            that same April

& issued
        what was known as
            the St. Louis Resolution—

"We call upon the
        workers of all countries

to refuse support
  to their governments
    in their wars."

Some were sympathetic
  to the stong socialist and
    union movements in Germany

in a struggle
    against
      Czarist barbarism—

others felt it
  was just a distracting disturbance
      between Russian
        & German militaries.

The Lower East Side was split.
  The pressure to support
    their new country

was great—not that pogroms
    by the Brooklyn Bridge were feared
  though the dirk-tined rioting peasant's rake
    was not that far
      in the past.

The Wilson administration
  generated war hysteria

Scott Nearing, Eugene Debs
      went to jail

The government threatened
the mailing rights of the *Jewish Daily Forward*
and other socialist papers
opposing the war.

Then
the climate was different
after the war.

There was hideous inflation
and F.O.B.
    Fear of Bolsheviks—

and many mayhemic forces
were set against the
Lower East Side socialist zone.

The anti-red hysteria was nationwide
The Wobblies were crushed
The strikers of Seattle crushed
The Palmer Raids
Federal troops used to club down
                honest dispute
Emma Goldman deported
Five socialists expelled from the
                N.Y. legislature
and the socialist Victor Berger
banned from his seat in the Congress.

There was a split in
the Socialist Party in 1919

& the birth of the Communist Party.

You think there was factionalism
in the 1960s—
The factions of 1920 hissed
like 35,000 ganders
        in an amanita valley—

and a democratic socialist
in the '20s and '30s
was wedged in pain among
the sharp-tongued Moscow leftists
and sharp-tongued bitter-shitter rightists.

Oh they failed
to spread the East Side zone
into a broader country
of psychopathic landboomers

& smug townies
who thought they could hog
the keys to the sky

There was the fact that
a climate of lectures and rallies
can aid in the first rough forward step,
            but rarely the second —

They knew with all the hurt of their years
how the socialist fervor fell —
and the failure of those
    who had seen the socialist dawn
to break it from sea to sea.

Most of them fled the rubbly slums,
and tens of thousands more,
for few there are
who joy
to live in dirt

They joked how the ships
brought the greenhorns to Rutgers Square
as the moving vans
took the radicals to the Bronx

        For most
        the game
        was to get OUT

        but for some
        like Congressman London
        the East Side
        was the
            world
        in which to stay

        He was there all his life
        till killed by a car
        as he crossed 2nd Avenue —

Shelley had Keats in his pocket
London had Chekhov.

Oh they failed
but I can hear their ghosts
walk down the cobbles
outside the St. Mark's Church

the poets, the strikers, the printers,
the firebrands, the leafleteers—
comrades when the word had its glow—

with a passion for justice
        that never fades away
though heartbreak
        to know
                that they had failed

to make a New World
inside the New World
at century's turn
They were the Yiddish-speaking socialists
of the Lower East Side.

THE PLANE

The plane
flies over
the lakes
in the pine barrens

& the moon
gleams
suddenly
on each

like a quick
flash—

it's startling.

      the 3-quarter
moon
up there like
a mail sack
full of pleasure

pond 'pon pond

till it stops
& I feel

a longing
to see more

pondic
lun' flash!

more! more!

           Flying from Detroit
           to Albany
           October 5, 1984

YOUR BREATH

Your breath
upon the pillow's lace

was like the wake
of a hummingbird's wings

on the wild columbine

THE CHAIN

For 15-thousand years
the plutonium
in the smoke detector
lay in the Woodstock dump

till the day
the grade-blader scraped it out
& smashed it to chiplets
the chipmunk pulled
to the pouch of his cheeks

& during
the next 200
             years

it caused
        6 cancers

in a skunk
a crow   a deer
a dog   a dog
and Johnny McQuaife

THE TIME OF PERF-PO

Some people stand on stilts
and chant Akkadian verse

while others smear marmalade
      with a pleasing sibilant slush
on transducer-dappled basketballs

as they crouch in a whirling barrel
and sing random phonemes
            flashed on a screen

to end the war

Oh they gather their muses together—
roller skates and bells! slides and synths!
computers and masks! monkeys and fever!
donuts and drums!

The time of perf-po is now
The time of perf-po is now

There is a Muse of Combinations
And a Muse called Retentia
            that Freezes Time

And a Muse
that helps you create
      a 4-dimensional poem zone

These are the Muses of Perf-Po

The Muse of Combinations
helps you to gather
your greatest skills
            in the poem zone

Retentia captures the Image
            and helps you array it

on tape and type, film and chip

There's a painting that shows
an Egyptian goddess
pouring a shower of tiger lilies
down upon those before her

Such is the shower
          in the 4-D poem zone

          The time of perf-po is now
          The time of perf-po is now

How beautiful is the
               unification
of word & melody   throb & vision
sky & thrill   perf & joy

in the 4-dimensional poem zone

All the components that
Aristotle listed:
Plot, Diction, Character, Meter/Melody,
Thought and Spectacle

fly into the zone

with Music, Motion, Logos,
          Percussion, Bird Songs,
          Clogs, Images,
          Story & Theme Events

          & speckle-throated lilies
               soft on the face

          The time of perf-po is now
          The time of perf-po is now

I hunger for thee
O perf-po

I yearn for a rinse of nonsense
to click upon my ears

I seethe for the undisappointed dash
of vowels & dithyrambs

I cry for a moan zone
of eery eeryismus

I know
that the words must
star in the mix

and I scheme with every cortical curl
to honor the sonnet, the breath, the bee, and the lyre

but I hunger for thee
O perf-po

And the time of perf-po is now
The time of perf-po is now

Some bards cast a
Mallarménean mystery,
vast as arctic flowers,
out over the poem zone

and those who believe in the soul
might try to startle the zone
with a séance of surds
to set free Dante's ghost
or the haint of Ibsen
of Gloucester's doves

We are talking in perf-tongues
We are calling down the Images

And the time of perf-po is now
The time of perf-po is now

The future of perf
    is measured in parsecs

I see the asteroid belt lit up
for a perf-po exhibit

I see the colors of stars being changed
to form a blinking of words

I see Li Po's poems
painted on giant masts
and flung into the sun

I see the seven Harmonists
standing on Plato's seven
            celestial circles

singing the
            Cincinnati phone directory

for the
Time of perf-po is now
The time of perf-po is now

The impulse
    gnaws like a deer mouse
            under the porch

with its own terminology:

perf-o-lalia

    the tendency to conduct

your personal affairs
as if they were a
perf-po concert

perf-o-mancy

the art of divining the future
with perf-po

perf-o-path

one who commits crimes
through perf-po

astro-perf

the tendency to view
the workings of the universe
as perf-po

The time of perf-po is now
The time of perf-po is now

The rules of perfo-po
would chew up a grove
of pulp pine

but here are some from Volume I:

1. If you are going to recite
sonnets on roller skates
wear knee pads

2. Never neglect
the toil over words

3. Figure out the
mix of your muses

4. Do not forget you
can Dance for Joy

while weeping
(or party while suffering)

5. Never let the
    audience get too
    warm

6. Make sure the stitches
    are part of the beauty

7. Do not neglect the
    concept of
    perf-po videos

8. Bring a skate key
    (while you're making a better world)

The time of perf-po is now
The time of perf-po is now

I wanted to be a part
of the time
that healed the hatred

The spectacle of perf
vanishes
poofs
flees
evaporates

and all that is left

is a jagged
clip of an ad,
a tape, some slides,
perhaps a video,
a set list, tired feet,
some perf notes,

twisted memories,

      & tiger lilies
      swept in a bag.

Yet tomorrow we
      fly to another city

hoping to find eternity

realign our muses
set up another poem zone

a jumble
of ladders
to reach
us over
the
walls

CIRCLES OF ICE

The woolly white dog named Roshi
lay
   on the gray snow bank
by the flappy-barked yellow birch
        next to the sap house

as we trudged into the forest
to empty the buckets.

In each a chilly discus of sap ice
floats
to be flung away
        as we pour.
Most fall down with a crackly thud
and flick flecks of sap on our boots
but a few land on their edges
and roll down the hill.

Sometimes that's
        what life seems like—
circles of ice
rolling down a hill

but not today,
for you can lean at the edge
of the freshly emptied sugarbush
and listen
        to the perf-sap

that is, to the subtle sounds
of sap-drips
        plinking the pails.

Tom has an idea for a musical instrument—
You record the various drips
and put them on chips

A Sap Lyre

The Tambourine for the hay field
The Panpipes for the vineyard
The Sap Lyre for the sugarbush.

Back in the sugar house
we wadded the *New York Times*
and tossed it into the metal mouth
of the Small Brothers boiler

"Reagan Kills Farm Aid" was
the head of the first page aflame.

It wasn't many minutes of hurling
the six-foot slabs in the firebox
till Tom Bryan was pouring
the first few gallons
through filtering funnels of cloth

and woolly Roshi waited
with the eagerness
of 20,000,000 years
for Tom to pour her a
taste in a jar lid

and the circles of ice
roll down the hill.

April 1985

HYMN TO ARCHILOCHUS

For Joe Cardarelli

On the rocky isle of Paros*
    2700 years ago
        was born a bard
who smote the strings of his lyre
    with a newness
        that made them gasp
           for a thousand years

His name was Archilochus
He was thought by the ancients
        the equal of Homer
The halves of his brain
    shared secrets by the billion
        to make it new.

From Plutarch†
we learn that Archilochus
made many inventions:

the ithyphallic trochaic trimeter
the recitative
    (rhythmical recitation
        of poetry to the lyre or flute)
the combination of unlike measures
the epode
    (long line followed by short)
the tetrameter
the cretic
the prosodiac
the combination of epibatic paeon with the iambic
the lengthened "heroic" with prosodiac and cretic
the concept of singing and recitation
        within the same poem

*One of the Cyclades Islands southeast of Athens.
†*On Music.*

and he was the first to tune his lyre
          an octave higher than his voice

He wrote the
     victory song
          at the Olympics

In later centuries
          they used to
               stitch together
a rhapsody

               of his poems & songs
               & tour the islands
     doing
          A Night of Archilochus.

He was the first great confessional poet
They spoke of his raging iambics
He was engaged to a woman named Neobule
but her father intervened
               and prevented it
and he wrote about him
               with such a bitter pulse
that the verses
          were said to cause a suicide

Critics accused Archilochus of
"slandering himself"
because, through his poesy,
people down the centuries
knew he was the son of a slave woman, Enipo,
that pov drove him from Paros to Thasos*
that he was adulterous & lecherous.

He was the first of the poets
          to de-macho his art

*Island off the coast of Thrace.

Once he let them strip away his shield
        on the field of battle
and laughed of it later in trochees & dactyls*

an act that got him thrown
        out of Sparta—
            The South Africa
            of 600 B.C.

What an honor
        when the Spartan secret police
ordered his books removed
for erotolalia.

He was a mercenary
        as well as a bard
He must have looked like a samurai
        standing on the marble chips
                        of Paros
            with greaves on the legs
        & a horsehair plume on his helmet

his tortoise-shell lyre packed away
                        with his poems
            in a sheepskin satchel.

        O bards
        ponder Archilochus
            you who think,
                "Hey, my poems are going to last
                all the way till the Milky Way
                explodes."

        Your archives
            bulging in acid-free binders
                at U.C.-San Diego

*Ἀσπίδι μὲν Σαΐων τις ἀγάλλεται, ἣν παρὰ θάμνῳ
    ἔντος ἀμώμητον κάλλιπον οὐκ ἐθέλων
ἄυτον δ'ἐκ μ'ἐσάωσα τίμοι μέλει ἀσπὶς ἐκείνη;
    ἐρρέτω. ἐξαυτις κτήσομαι οὐ κακίω

and a staff
of graduate students
sorting them clean!

The fireman felt the wall
above my bed
just where I'd taped
a quote from a poem
by Robert Kelly.

On the blanket were all of the books
of Charles Olson

and my notes for
the Olson Memorial lectures

when I was
wounded by fire in
the frothsome night

"Why are you saving those books?"
the fireman asked
pointing his ax
toward the stereo

hosing down my wall of verse
and chopping the plaster.

As I scooped up the books
I thought of Archilochus

whose work comes down to us
in pitiful tatters

gone
 shredded
 stomped
 abyssed

gone with the fires

that burned Alexandria
gone with the disrepute
                & disrespect
gone with the book-burning frenzy
                of Christians and Moslems
gone with the mold spores
        alighting atop the
                long chains of molecules
                        holding the structure of paper

                for a thousand-year lunch
                        of the lines of Archilochus

                The first large magnetic body
                that passes too close to earth
                will erase the tapes
                The one that crashes
                        will burn the books

                and the sky shall spit
                        your poems out
                                like pellets of fire

The home town of Catullus
                was Verona
where they saved a single manuscript
but no one saved Archilochus.

Your wounded verses sing
across the ages
                O Archilochus

I can see you standing
                on a hillside
holding your 4-string lyre
and how you were an inventer!

striking the twisted strings
on the palmwood sounding board
      with a limberlimbic meter
         whose waves
            slosh gently
and faintly
all the way to my burning wall,

and it was you who said
ἐι γὰρ ὡς ἐμοὶ γένοιτο χειρα Νεοβόυλης Φιγειν
"if only it could happen
      that I could touch
        the hand of Neobule"

      (*Sung*)

There used to be a poet named Archilochus
one of the greatest of them all
Oh there's nothing of his poetry now
except some scattered lines

I wish we could hear Archilochus
play his four-stringed lyre
Oh to hear some great poetry
to make the world entire

Oh I learned from Archilochus
about the Nightingale
Oh I long to hold the nightingale
nesting in my hands

and I love to spend the Catskill spring
the Catskill spring with you
but you know that there's a hunger there
to touch the nightingale

Oh they talk so elegantly
about eternity
Oh I sing to you Archilochus
to touch the nightingale &

feel those flashing feathers
          on my fingertips &
feel the fluttering wings
          upon my begging lips

ἀηδονιδέυς

NOTES

POEM FROM JAIL (page 3)
There were eight of us in three boats, one of them bearing a large dark banner with white letters, ACTION FOR LIFE. We started from a dock in New London, Connecticut, and rowed across New London harbor toward the opposite shore at Groton, where the General Dynamic Corporation's Electric Boat Shipyard was building Polaris nuclear submarines.

It was August 8, 1961, the day for the commissioning of the *Ethan Allen*, a Polaris sub carrying sixteen nuclear missiles. In the days previous, we had conducted vigils in a canoe near the sub and had seen on the docks the Polaris missiles surrounded by cranes and girders, ready to be loaded — enough, we calculated, to kill about thirty million people. Homer called Odysseus the "sacker of cities," but these missiles were, and are, the true sackers, for each was aimed, we had read, at a specific Russian or Chinese city.

We knew from experience that the Coast Guard cutters would try to block our approach to the submarine. We could see frogmen on the decks ready to jump into the water and intercept us. Our plan was to advance as far as we could, then dive from our boats and swim toward the sub. We had trained for it. During the summer we'd played "frogmen vs. pacifists" at a nearby lake, practicing nonviolent tactics to elude the Navy swimmers. I was wearing my custard-colored swimming suit with an Eye of Horus inked upon the tiny front pocket containing my ear plugs and thirty-five cents, with which to make phone calls upon arrest.

It was not certain what would have occurred had I crawled aboard the *Ethan Allen* that August day. Others who had actually touched or boarded Polaris submarines during demonstrations had been given federal-prison terms. If you were caught on the way, you were usually merely held until the launching or commissioning ceremonies were concluded and then set free. We were determined to get arrested.

All of us had prepared personal statements on the Action for Life, which were printed and handed out. In mine I wrote, "I plan to spend the next six or seven months aboard the *Ethan Allen* as a permanent fixture of love and to maintain a preventative vigil on the missile hatches."

As we approached the long dock where the sub was parked, we were blocked by several Coast Guard boats and by what appeared to be a green tugboat. The latter was swarming with men, apparently shipyard workers deputized for the day. We dove into the chilly water and did our best Olympic crawls toward the goal. Plop plop plop all around us the men jumped from the tugboat, some attired only in rolled-up pants. I was apprehended almost at once and hauled up the rough sides of the tug with scrapes of ouch.

On the deck I was held by a burly guy with dripping pants. "Okay, okay," I said. "I give up. Just tell me where to stand."

"Stand over there," he replied, pointing to the other edge of the barge, only about a hundred yards from the *Ethan Allen*. He released me at the same time, so I sprinted to the railing and dived back into the water.

I gave it the fastest crawl in pacifist history. If I'd had flippers, I'd have made it. About a hundred feet from the sub, the green boat literally ran me down and came to a halt by the dock. I went under water as far as I could, pushing away from it, worried that the propellers might treat me like a shirt in a washing machine. When I surfaced, there was again the plop plop of humans from the boat. This time they tied me with ropes.

Just like past attempts to board the subs, we were kept till after the ceremonies, then set free. We banded together and went around to the front of the shipyard and held a sit-in, blocking the gate. We were arrested and convicted for breach of the peace and resisting arrest. I refused to walk to my cell and was half-dragged, half-carried there, one of the officers using my hair as a handle. We were given a fine of $150, which none of us paid, so we were sent back to jail to sit it off at two dollars per day, a sentence of seventy-five days.

Rock-and-roll was played all the time, but paper, pencils, and newspapers were taboo, as were news broadcasts. They switched off the radio through the speakers when news was imminent. They refused me my Egyptian grammar and a book on Greek metrics, the guard muttering something about a "Russian code book," and I had to fast for a day to get them. I acquired a contraband pencil and began to write "Poem from Jail" on long lengths of toilet paper. The lines were kept short because of to the narrowness of the writing surface. For two weeks I worked on the poem, hiding rolled wads of tissue under my mattress or on crossbars near the ceiling. I cut oblong sections from the inside of cigarette packs and made a copy.

At the time I was researching four main subjects: pacifist theory, Egyptian hieroglyphics, Greek meters, and Hesiod's *Theogony*. I had taken a course in Hesiod and had the genealogy of the Greek gods clearly in mind, so I could write with assurance in the poem, for instance, that Zeus was the grandnephew of the Spectres of Vengeance. I studied Egyptian in my cell by making flash cards. I carefully drew the hieroglyphs individually on small squares of cigarette-pack inner linings and then wrote the phonetic sound and translation on the back. I was also very much interested in Greek meters and myths. As I wrote "Poem from Jail," I would stare at the scroll of toilet paper upon my bunk and visualize or "auralize" a specific meter, then summon the words to fill it. Thus I experienced the thrill, say, of my first Ionic a minore, $\cup\cup\acute{-}-$, or epitrite, $\acute{-}\cup\bar{-}-$.

We were a constant trouble to the authorities. One of us started a secret pass-around prison newspaper. There were support demonstrations of pacifists outside the jail we'd hear about through scuttlebutt. Even though we were prepared for the full seventy-five days, after two weeks they told us to get our stuff packed and ready to move.

It was totally unexpected. We were in the middle of a poker game. I realized "Poem from Jail" would surely be confiscated. Once before, there had been a search of prisoners in the recreation room. It was only by passing the rather thick wad of cigarette wrappers under a table to brother pacifist Dave Mitchell, who had already been searched, that "Poem from Jail" had been saved.

While the guard waited for me to pack, I acted upset, saying that I guessed I wouldn't be able to take my poetry with me. I made a show of flushing about fifty feet of verse. Then, outside his ken, I stuffed the second copy under the innersole of my tennis shoe. I could barely get my foot back in the shoe. I was sure it was as conspicuous as a clubfoot. Sure enough, before we left, they opened my Egyptian grammar and removed what writings they found, but they did not peek in my shoes, and I escaped jubilantly with my poem.

There was a Peacemakers' conference at the Polaris Action farm, where we lived during that summer, after our release from jail. I typed up "Poem from Jail" and showed it to several friends at the conference, notably Jean Morton Forest and Allen Hoffman, who urged me to publish it. It was my first work, after years of search, that I felt fit in with the best of my generation. I sent it to Lawrence Ferlinghetti, who, to my lasting gratitude, printed it as a City Lights publication.

(page 4-5)
The failure of Stassen; the Teller intervention; Radford wailing for death; Madame Chiang Kai-shek; the retreat of MacArthur and the hidden history of the Korean War—see I.F. Stone's book *The Hidden History of the Korean War.*

(pages 14-15)

> O Zeus
> Great-grandson
> of the earth,
> O Zeus,
> third generation
> from Chaos,
> O Zeus,
> grandnephew
> of the
> Spectres of Vengeance!

Zeus can be considered the great-grandson of Gaia, since Gaia gave birth to Ouranos (Uranus), who was the father of Kronos, who was the father of Zeus—hence great-grandson. On the other hand, since Gaia mated with her offspring, Ouranus, to produce Kronos, Zeus could also be considered a grandson of Gaia. As for Zeus being third generation from Chaos, I have interpreted lines 116-117 of the *Theogony* to imply that Gaia came out of the primal Chaos. The Furies, or Spectres of Vengeance, it will be recalled, were born of Gaia when she received the blood of Kronos within her— hence Zeus as grandnephew of the Spectres. Or perhaps it would be proper instead to assert Zeus the *great*-grandnephew of the Spectres of Vengeance. It was a long time ago.

CEMETERY HILL (page 31)
Part One was written in late 1961 while I was living in a peace commune on East Thirty-Eighth Street. The arrayal of lines was inspired by John Cage's *Silence*, especially the works "Lecture on Nothing" and "Composition as Process."

PRAYER FOR THE UNITY OF THE EYE (page 44)
This poem in celebration of healing uses elements of the Isis-Osiris legends, combining them with memories of my mother when I was a child massaging my forehead to ease away headaches. Horus, son of Isis and Osiris, had soared aloft on his hawk wings to battle Set, after Set had killed Osiris. Horus's eye was gouged out. Later the pieces of the Eye of Horus were restored by Isis and the knowledge god Thoth, as an example of the precept that "the restitution of the Oculus is the foundation of theology."

PINDAR'S REVENGE (page 45)
The epigraph, Ἄριστον μὲν ὕδωρ, is the opening half-line of Pindar's First Olympian Ode. *Ariston men hudor* may be translated as 'water is the greatest thing.' Regarding Pindar's revenge, see the inscription on John Keats's tomb.

SHEEP-FUCK POEM (page 49)
This poem was inspired by B.R., secret oviphile of Jackson County, for I never actually conjoined with a baa-baa, ma, you gotta believe me!

THIS IS THE PRAYER WHEEL & VISION (page 50)
I continued studying Egyptian in late 1961 after I had written "Poem From Jail." I was living at 509 East Eleventh. It was about two months before I would found *Fuck You/A Magazine of the Arts*. I passed a meat store on First Avenue around Twelfth Street, and I was amazed by the window. There, resting upon white paper in a flat tray was half of a cow's head, stripped of skin, with a huge eye staring up. It had the effect of a religious revelation. The phrase *Peace Eye* came into my mind. I was much taken at the time with the Eye of Horus, 𓂀 , and with Egyptian religion in general. Within weeks, I had written a series of poems outlining my view of Peace Eye, some of which I wrote in jail after a sit-in at the New York Atomic Energy Commission protesting atmospheric nuclear

tests (see the story, "The A.E.C. Sit-In" in *Tales of Beatnik Glory*, Vol. I. Readers who want to view the entire Peace Eye series may consult my book *Peace Eye*, published in 1966.

ELM-FUCK POEM (page 51)
When I was about eight years old, there was an elm tree next to the sand pile in the back yard where I loved to sit on summer days building tiny arenaceous structures and roadways. About three feet above the sand pile, where the two halves of the elm tree's trunk forked apart, what I took to be sap would sometimes flow. I used to climb the tree, with its juices flowing in a slow warm runnel from that lowest crotch. There could have been a coda to this poem, on the highly fulfilling sensation of placing one's bare foot into the wet elm V, and then to lift upward, shifting the body's weight upon the foot in the wet V, as the first act in climbing it.

HOLY WAS DEMETER WALKING TH'CORN FURROW (page 54)
Demeter was walking the earth, looking for the kidnapped Persephone. She was pursued by Poseidon and changed herself into a mare. Poseidon changed into a stallion, and Demeter was unable to escape. The product of their union was the horse Areion and a daughter called Despoina. Demeter was at first enraged (Demeter Ἐρινύς) but later calmed down and washed herself in the river Ladon. The epithet for Demeter, λουσία, refers to Demeter the Washed, from the verb λούω, 'to bathe.' There is a cave in Arcadia, apparently extant, called Mavrospelyia, or Dark Cave, where Demeter Μέλαινα, the Dark, clad in black, was supposed to have retired in a mixture of mourning for Persephone and anger at Poseidon. What a cave some day to visit. The poem in this book, however, is not of Demeter the Sad but of the Demeter who once lay down in an ancient field with Iasion, a mere grateful mortal of no special claim. Da-Mater and Deo are names for Demeter.

THE V.F.W. CRAWLING CONTEST (page 61)
For years I had wanted to write this poem of the long, groaning road. It was sort of a secular version of the rather more mystic crawl at the end of "Poem from Jail." I began "The V.F.W. Crawling Contest" a few weeks after finishing my book on the Manson group, which had been a grueling and grim eighteen-month project. That, the horrid continuation of the Vietnam war, the depreda-

tions of Nixon, and the breakup of my rock band all combined to
impel this poem of 1971.

THE ICE (page 84)
This true tale was composed in 1973 and was one of the first acts
toward the creation of *Tales of Beatnik Glory*, in the story "The
Mother-in-Law."

STAND BY MY SIDE, O LORD (page 85)
In 1973 when I began work on *Tales of Beatnik Glory*, I also began
a book of verse, *Egyptian Hieroglyphics*. Hence the reference in
this poem to the "lives/of the hieroglyphic/artists," which I was
studying in preparation for the book.

EGYPTIAN HIEROGLYPHICS (page 87)
This series of poems was published in 1974 by Albert Glover in one
volume of a twenty-eight-part Curriculum of the Soul, conceived by
John Clark and Albert Glover from the poem "A Plan for a Cur-
riculum of the Soul," by Charles Olson. Categories for the cur-
riculum as listed in Olson's poem, such as Egyptian Hieroglyphics,
were taken on by individual writers.

AB-MER (page 89)
"Ab-Mer" was inspired by researches into possible artistic rebellion
in the rather totalitarian milieu of ancient Egypt. I was looking for
Lost Generations, for sistra-shaking Dadaists in tent towns on the
edge of half-finished pyramids, for cubists in basalt, for free-speech
movements on papyrus. And while the record is fairly barren of
such movements, I did discover some hints of it. I set the poem in-
side a rebel art school, one of the "Houses of Hathor," during the
reign of Ammenemes I, about 1985 B.C. It is a love story involving
Ab-Mer, a freedom-loving painter, and the dancer I-mm-eti.

HIEROGLYPHS (page 99)
"Hieroglyphs" analyzes the belief that the hieroglyphs painted and
carved on funerary items *actually were alive*! In addition, there
were the Soul Scrolls, rolls of painted papyrus found in coffins in
Thebes around 1100 B.C. These beautiful scrolls trace the stages of
transmigration and initiation for the deceased on the way to
purification, judgment, and enternity. Readers may want to

examine the two-volume set *Mythological Papyri*, translated by Alexandre Piankoff and published by Pantheon in the Bollingen Series, Vol. I, plates of the Soul Scrolls printed on long narrow rectangles of paper; Vol. II, texts and exegesis.

I WANT TO BE PURIFIED (page 101)
In "I Want to Be Purified," the Chantress of Amon, a woman named Her-Wetet, is eager to jump into the Lake of Fire purification glyph, an integral part of the Egyptian post-thanatos subterranean vision. In the Soul Scrolls, the Lake of Fire is presented as a square bordered by a courtyard protected by four fire apes. In some of the paintings the fire apes hold torches, which they douse in pails of milk. (See "Cemetery Hill" (page 164) for use of this pail-stub image). After the broil in the lake came judgment and journey to the fields of paradise, the so-called Yaru Fields. Interesting Lakes of Fire are to be found on Soul Scrolls 5, 8, and 18 in *Mythological Papyri*.

BOOTY (page 106)
"Booty" traces a team of Egyptian graverobbers, the Mek-Macraes, who for decades had attempted to rob the cunningly booby-trapped tomb of Her-Wetet, Chantress of Amon. Her-Wetet was a musician-singer associated with the temple of Amon, the chief deity of Thebes. With an ingenius wooden probe the Mek-Macraes manage to rob the grave, and when they pry the ruby eyes from a statue of Her-Wetet, they enact the results predicted in the poem "Hieroglyphs," so that there is a corresponding injury to her actual eyes as she resides in the paradisiacal Yaru Fields.

REPORT (page 111)
In "Report: Council of Eye-Forms Data Squad," I wanted to outline some Egyptian burial techniques and a sense of the religious ceremonies performed for chantress Her-Wetet as she strode through the stages of purification and judgment. For "The Council of Eye Forms" see the notes below.

20,000 A.D. (page 121)
In "20,000 A.D.," I wanted to bring a science-fiction aspect to "Egyptian Hieroglyphics," so I posited the existence in A.D. 20,000 of a "superemanated civilization" consistiong of hiero-brain-

spheres, the Council of Eye Forms, a vast, interconnected, galaxy-wide set of minds, freed from the flesh, extremely powerful, virtually eternal, meditative, kind, and loving. Against them is set the Egyptian god Apopis, or Apep, itself a galaxy-sized evil demon that is an eater of light; that is, each morning it seeks to devour the sun in the sun barge as it crosseth the sky. The poem's plot supposes "What if a way existed to kill Apopis once and for all?" Would the Council of Eye Forms go for it? Or would they go through a classic galactic liberal lame-out and stall so long, debating and indecisive, that the moment would be lost and Apopis unfreeze itself (where it had been caught by the Eye Forms) and wiggle away in shrieks of light-eating laughter?

HOMAGE TO LOVE-ZAP (page 131)
The term *love-zap* was created by Julian Beck and Judith Malina of the Living Theater. It denotes the outward-acting power of concentrated love as a beam that can act to overcome injustice and evil, especially when applied at the barricades. It is important for love-zap to be recognized as a Forward Acting Thing, as opposed to the so-called redemptive power of unearned suffering described by Martin King. The concept of concerted love-zap assumes the Shelleyan belief that the *will* of the species can overcome evil: the ahimsa arc strike, guerrilla lovefare from those few who dare to organize others to confront at the barricades.

THE AGE (page 137)
This was written in very late 1975 to be read at the New Year's Day gathering at the St. Mark's Church in New York City. At the time I was conducting researches into the domestic activities of U.S. intelligence services and secret police. There were a number of public investigations by Congress in the years after the fall of Nixon, and it looked for a while as if the assassination of the 1960s might be explicated.

LOVE & THE FALLING IRON (page 146)

> Charles O.: to beg a chapel
> once again in which
> to pray thy safety's sake
> on the airline of the
>
> falling iron

refs to a visit to Olson in late 1969 at New York Hospital, and then, as we left, we went into the chapel, Susan Cohen and I, for a prayer to guide him to safety. The "falling iron" refers to Hesiod's anvil.

SAPPHO'S POEM BEGINNING Φαίνεταί μοι (page 150)
In the summer of 1977 I sang some Sappho in the Greek to Allen Ginsberg, who encouraged me to sing Sapph' at a poetry reading I was to give that night. I did, and the response was enthusiastic. Thus began a course of years that extends to this day of inventing musical instruments to facilitate the recitation of my verse. I have created the bardic Pulse Lyre, (see drawing on page 193), the Talking Tie, the Light Lyre, and other devices that supply soft percussive and melodic support, which in no way can overwhelm the words. A number of poems in this volume were created to be accompanied by my instruments. They include the poem by Sappho, "Yiddish-Speaking Socialists of the Lower East Side," "The Time of Perf-Po," "Hymn to Archilochus," and "The Cutting Prow." Sappho's poem here translated is one of the most beautiful love poems in any language, and I join a long list of poets, including Catullus and Byron, who have brought it to their own.

HYMN TO O (page 154)
τὸ ἄπειρον , toh ápayron, is the alpha-privative noun from the verb περάω or πείρω — 'to pierce quite through, to drive right across'— and was Anaximander's term for the ἀρχή, that is, the primal stuff, the Urstoff, the unpierceable, uncrossable universal mush gush. You will recall the deep-image poetry movement of the late 1950s and early 1960s. Anaximander's τὸ ἄπειρον burned itself into the mind that way: Galactic Image. The anvil fell nine days and nights to get into Tartarus. The Boat slides forever trying to cross the seas of Apeiron.

SAPPHO ON EAST SEVENTH (page 166)
During the summer and early fall of 1982, I wrote this sho-sto-po about the 1963 visit of the ghost of Sappho to a poet in the Lower East Side of New York City. This story poem is central to Volume II of *Tales of Beatnik Glory*, where it also will be found. See the

stories "A Night at the Café Perf-Po" and "Cynthia," in *Tales of Beatnik Glory*, Vol. II.

THE FIVE FEET (page 194)
One afternoon in the spring of 1984, Steven Taylor and I met at Allen Ginsberg's place on East Twelfth and wrote a tune to this, which we recorded in the Fugs reunion album, *Refuse to Be Burnt-Out*.

THE YIDDISH-SPEAKING SOCIALISTS OF THE LOWER EAST SIDE (page 205)
This poem, written to be accompanied by the Pulse Lyre, was written while researching the story "Farbrente Rose," in *Tales of Beatnik Glory*, Vol. II. The books below supplied much useful and thrilling information:

The House on Henry Street, Lillian Wald
Memoirs of a Revolutionary, Eva Broido
World of Our Fathers, Irving Howe
How the Other Half Lives, Jacob Riis
Labor and Farmer Parties in the United States, Nathan Fine
Born One Year Before the Twentieth Century, Minnie Fisher

THE TIME OF PERF-PO (page 218)
Steven Taylor and I have been creating a musical-dramatic version of the story in *Tales of Beatnik Glory*, Vol. II, entitled "A Night at the Café Perf-Po." The poem printed here is the opening section of the musical.

The coffee house of 17th-century England
was a place of fellowship where
ideas could be freely exchanged.
The turn-of-the-century Parisian cafes
witnessed the birth of cubism and surrealism.
The coffee houses of 1950s America
hosted poetry readings that continue to
influence literature and society.
We hope such a spirit
welcomes our readers in the pages of
Coffee House Press books.